WHAT WE STOOD FOR

*THE STORY OF A REVOLUTIONARY
BLACK WOMAN*

This book is a publication of
Diasporic Africa Press

New York | www.dafricapress.com

Copyright @ Deborah Jones and Thandisizwe Chimurenga 2024

All rights reserved. No part of this publication may be reproduced or distributed in any form or by any means, or stored in a database or retrieval system, without the prior written permission of the publisher.

Cover Photos: Photos for collage courtesy of the Los Angeles Times Photographic Archive, UCLA Library Special Collections.

Library of Congress Control Number: 2023951282

ISBN-13 978-1-937306-78-6 (pbk.: alk paper)

Ebook: 978-1-937306-79-3

WHAT WE STOOD FOR

THE STORY OF A REVOLUTIONARY BLACK WOMAN

DEBORAH JONES
with the assistance of Thandisizwe Chimurenga

DIASPORIC AFRICA PRESS

NEW YORK

1

PROLOGUE

I stumbled at first because I couldn't see. I thought there were needles in my eyes, but it was simply the sun. I wanted some cool water so badly, and my lips were so swollen. *If I could just get this taste of blood out of my mouth, I'll be alright*, I told myself.

"Keep one foot in front of the other," became like a silent mantra. That was all we had to do. Something so simple that it seemed almost Herculean. And then I would take a step.

One foot . . .

I was convinced my left foot was broken. It felt like a huge butcher knife was attempting to escape through it. My big toe throbbed.

. . . in front of the other.

It was Mother's Day, 1970. A typically beautiful and warm Sunday afternoon in LA. Idili, who was a couple of months younger, walked alongside me. She was short and petite and had a small, neatly shaped round Afro. When she smiled, you would think that she had captured the entire sun within her little frame. She wasn't smiling now, however, as we made our way up Century Blvd. in Inglewood. She also wasn't limping like me; her steps were slow, almost like she was asking permission. Her eyes, which were usually full of life, were wide and glass-like, never looking up from the ground beneath her. One side of her face was streaked with tears. On the other side of her face was a slender line of raw pink flesh, from where she had been burned with a soldering iron. *That's gonna get infected if we don't hurry up and get to a doctor,* I thought . . .

2

GENESIS

I heard voices, loud and excited, coming from inside the apartment. The door was slightly ajar, but I knocked hard to make sure they could hear me.

"Little girl, what do you want?" Ken asked when he came to the door. He was only fourteen but he acted so much older. Tall for his age, he wore glasses that, in my mind, made him look really smart. He was really smart, so the glasses weren't some kind of adornment. He was either always reading or always talking about what he had read and debating ideas like a professor lecturing to a group of hungry students. He got his love of learning from his mom, an English literature teacher at Edison Junior High, where I would be going in a few years. Ken's father was a dentist who worked what seemed like seven days a week. It seemed like there was always a house full of neighborhood kids in their household.

He knew why I was there, but I answered his question anyway. "I wanna learn," I told him. He smiled a row of perfect white teeth with a gap in the middle and let me in.

On this day the kids inside were arguing about some "kissing case" that was happening down south. Two little boys charged with rape? The NAACP? I squeezed my frame into a spot at the very end of the couch so I could soak it all up.

Two things that were a constant presence in the spacious living room overlooking San Pedro Street in South Central Los Angeles: kids and books. Photographs of Black history figures adorned the walls, and a stereo system in the middle of the room was surrounded with jazz records. Music was the third constant in the Seaton household. It was always playing, sometimes loud, sometimes low, to complement whatever folks were discussing. A bookshelf, full and bulging, stood in one corner of the living room, where more books spilled out into a stack on the floor. The little apartment was home to all sorts of books on all kinds of subjects: history, geography, astronomy, linguistics. Large, oversized art books could be found taking up space with slender volumes of African American literature and English poetry. Both Ken's parents loved reading, but it was his father who loved jazz music. We would crowd in the living room, talking about books or news or who did what at school, and Mr. Freeman would come in with a serious look on his face. "C'mere, let me show y'all something," he'd say. He would put on a Charlie Parker or Dizzy Gillespie record, close his eyes, and hold his head down with his hands pointing out different sections to us. "Hear that part?" he'd ask us, his eyes still closed.

We were all encouraged to read and the Seatons would let us borrow books. We had to make a promise to bring the books back and to give them a brief report on our opinion of what we had read in order to keep our "library privileges." It was the perfect atmosphere for someone who wanted to learn.

It was 1959 and that was how I first met Ken. I was nine years old.

I had been going to the Seatons' house for a while. I would go some days after school or before dinner, when it would get dark, and we'd have to be inside. I loved to read, and I loved seeing all the books in their home. It was because I loved to read that I could keep up with all the conversations going on at their house.

"How do you know some of the things you know?" Ken asked me one day. I told him, "I'm a reader and I'm an admirer of Malcolm X, and I know he was a nationalist, you know, an African nationalist, besides being from the Nation of Islam." And then he asked me, "How old are you?" I proudly answered him, "Nine. Nine-and-a-half." He was intrigued.

My family lived on the same street as the Seatons but on the opposite end of the block. His family was already there when we moved to the neighborhood about six years earlier. Our home was a two-bedroom duplex with a living room, kitchen, a service porch and one bathroom. I shared a bedroom with my two younger sisters. It was a bit cramped, but it was cozy, and it was home.

Our block was primarily row after row of single-family dwellings, with a couple of duplexes and one or two apartment buildings sprinkled in. Each house had a small front yard that the owners took care of. The backyards were small, and a few homes had one-car garages. Still others had only street parking available, and fruit trees dotted the fences that rimmed the alleyways throughout the neighborhood. My neighbors took pride in their homes. As kids on our way to school we would wave to the adults out sweeping their porches or removing trash from the street in front of their homes before they headed off to work. On Saturday mornings the sound of lawn mowers would fill up the neighborhood. Kids would wake up, do chores around the house, and then go out to play. And when you went outside to play, you dare not step on anyone's grass!

At that time, the neighborhood around Fremont High School, 76th and San Pedro Streets, was a hard-working, Black lower middle-class neighborhood. Everyone knew each other; the adults knew the children and the children knew the adults. For instance, there was McGarrety's

Café. The McGarretys had five children. Two of them, fraternal twins named Claudette and Claude, were a couple of years older than me. There was a neighborhood market owned by Asians. There was a Pentecostal church, which later became a Maoist community center for a while. They would sell Mao Tse Tung's Red Book and talk about Red Guard politics. I don't recall any liquor stores in the immediate area. Certainly not like it is today.

My name is Deborah Faye Jones, and I was born into this community on September 3, 1950.

My father told me, much later when I was older, that he'd had a premonition about me not long after I was born: "There's going to be trouble for her."

No one—not me, my father, my mother—could have ever imagined what kind of trouble.

My dad, Frank Jones, was from Homestead, Florida, but I don't know what year he was born. His father was Cuban; Spanish was my dad's first language, but he learned English early. He was a very light-skinned Black man. He was what they call "fair skinned," with straight black hair. His birth certificate said Negro, and he was often mistaken for Latino and sometimes white, but he'd let you know really quick that he was Black, fiercely Black and proud. He met my mother in New Orleans during World War II. The story goes that my dad was twenty-one years old and in the Army when he and some guys in his unit were at this club on leave. I think it was one of those USO clubs for soldiers. Anyway, those guys that my dad was with, they were planning on raping my mother. This was in 1943. She was fifteen years old. I don't know how or why or who gave her a job in a club at that age, but she was there and she was a beauty. These guys, these soldiers, apparently must have talked among themselves about what they planned on doing and my dad just happened to be with them.

I don't know if they were Black or white or what, but my dad stood in front of my mom and protected her from being raped. He wasn't having any of it. He told them they were not going to do that and then he told my mom, "You shouldn't be out here alone. I'm going to marry you. You settle down, find us a place." They got married that day. My dad went back to Germany, where he was stationed, and stayed there and finished his tour of duty. He would send money to my mom to help her out with the little place she had found. When he finally got out of the Army he came back to New Orleans. My dad didn't touch my mom (so I was told) until he got back from the service, and that's how they began a family, when I was born in 1950.

My dad's people settled in Florida. His mother, Gladys Jones, was a full-blooded Seminole. She had a reputation. Apparently, she was a drinker who couldn't hold her liquor. She was wild and tore up things, kinda on the crazy side; that's what I gathered.

I met her only one time here in Los Angeles. I was seventeen years old, and it was at a record hop at Fremont High School. She had come to California to see my dad, who was in prison at the time. She told me she was a descendant of Osceola, the Seminole chief. She said she was from one of the Five Civilized Tribes but that she wasn't an "Indian." "Indians are from India," she said to me. "We never signed a peace treaty with the white man," she continued. "We always had slaves to escape to Florida. The powers that be took us to be slaves in Europe." I never saw my grandmother again after that. But her words have remained with me all this time.

My dad's father came from Cuba and ended up in Homestead. That's how he ended up meeting my grandmother. I don't know what his name was or what happened to him, but something happened to him because Jones is my father's adopted name. I only have pieces of that story.

Both my parents really weren't into telling me their family history too much, and I always thought that was strange. But the few things I was able to piece together was that my dad was adopted by a full-blooded African whose name was Jones in Homestead, when that man married my grandmother, Gladys.

From what I was told, I think her mother sold her at age nine to this Cuban man and she had three kids by him. They all came to Homestead, the older man and my grandmother and the three kids. After that she ended up with a Mr. Jones, and he adopted all three of her children.

My dad, Frank Jones, was a lot of things. A lot. He was multitasking before that was even a word. He was an intellectual. He spoke Spanish as well as four other languages. He had a degree in theology; he was an electrician; he owned a small grocery store. And he was also one of California's largest marijuana dealers. My father was gifted, but he was also troubled. He was a diagnosed paranoid schizophrenic.

My dad would tell war stories from when he was in Germany, but because of his challenges I wasn't quite sure how truthful his tales were. They sounded so fantastic to me. Later on, I found out that he had gone absent without leave (AWOL) during the war and had gone to Mexico and was selling weed. According to my mom, he was caught and put in the brig, but somehow still managed to get an honorable discharge after doing a three-year tour. While he was in Mexico he'd made numerous contacts, and that's how he began to deal marijuana once he got to California. Today, he'd probably own a bunch of dispensaries and farms and all of that. But back then that was a no-no.

Despite that, my parents didn't smoke marijuana. We never even smelled it as children. There were no illegal drugs in our family. There was no kind of addiction. My father never mentioned marijuana to us. He kept us out of it totally. As a matter of fact, when I told my parents I was smoking marijuana, which didn't start until I was in my twenties, they were relieved, like, "Whew... good!" They had seen what LSD and heroin had done to people. They were actually kind of happy.

The grocery my dad owned was over in Downey, southeast of Los Angeles. At that time, white folks really didn't want us to cross over into areas like South Gate, Downey, Lynwood. Even Compton was all white. They wanted to keep us away from those areas, but my sisters and I were these little Black kids with my dad, who is fair with straight hair, so they didn't quite know what to make of that. But that's not how we were brought up anyway. My dad told us, "You are Californians, you can go anywhere you want to go. This world belongs to you."

"There's a world out there," my mother used to say, "and we want you guys to enjoy it."

Looking back, I suspect that my father's personality, in addition to the light-skin privilege he possessed, are what cemented his attitude.

Once, when I was at Edison Junior High School, a foreign language teacher asked me to have a cigarette with her. I thought that was odd, even though I didn't smoke like some of the other kids. We all knew kids weren't allowed to smoke at school or else we'd get in trouble. After that teacher, a white woman, approached me a second time and asked me to come to her home. I told my parents, and my dad went to the school. I don't know what he said and who he said it to, but I was taken out of that class, and I never saw that white woman again.

My mom told me a story once, one that my dad had told her about his mother. One of his sisters was raped when she was thirteen years old. A man was in the actual act of raping her when my grandmother caught him. She grabbed a shotgun and shot him while he was on top of my aunt. Of course, she could've killed her own daughter; I guess she was just so enraged she hadn't stopped to think about that. But she shot him and killed him. Then she told my dad and his brother to take the man's body to the railroad tracks so that the train could run over it.

That's my dad's side of the family.

My mom, Mildred Faye Stone, was born February 10, 1928, in New Orleans, Louisiana. She had eleven brothers and sisters, but I only met one of her siblings. I know very little about either of my grandparents or great grandparents, or any of that. The only thing that I could piece together is that my mom left home early. She was considered the "Black girl" of the group. She said they actually called her "Black gal." And Louisiana is really funny when it comes to skin color. Octoroon this, quadroon that and all. She was called "Black gal" by her siblings and her grandmother, and they treated her differently, so she had this animosity, I'm assuming, from her own childhood.

I don't know any cousins, uncles, or aunties on either side of my family. The only family I ever knew was my mother, my father, my two sisters, and my father's mother, the one grandmother who I met only once. I don't really know her.

My mom was underage when my parents were married. She had no parents or guardians to okay it or say no. Her mother, my maternal grandmother, died giving birth to her. My mom was next to the youngest of eleven children. After her mom died, her dad, whose name I don't even remember, married another woman and had one more child. I don't know what happened to that woman he married, whether she died, or they divorced, or if she just left. My mom's dad worked for the state of Louisiana and supported this big ole family without remarrying, but he was a gambler and a womanizer. They had a big, beautiful home and all of that. My grandfather raised my mom along with his mother and his grandfather and the ten other siblings. I only knew one of my mom's siblings, a sister named Lula Mae, and I only met her briefly when I was about three or four years old. We just happened to go to Tennessee and my mom took these pictures of me, my aunt, and my cousins. And after that I never saw any of them again.

My mom's mother, my maternal grandmother, had obviously been a dark-skinned woman because my mother was dark brown. I don't know anything about her mother's background. She just wouldn't talk about it.

My mom came to San Francisco, California, with two of her best friends. And not knowing anything about life in the brand-new big city, it seemed exciting because they were young. But my mother always had the wisdom to know what was good for her and what was not. Eventually, her two friends got caught up with some pimps, but not my mom. She didn't fall for the okey-doke. She stayed there a while, and then she came down to Southern California and settled down while her friends stayed up north where they prostituted themselves and got hooked on heroin.

My father hadn't yet come to join her. I don't know where he was, and I never got the story. When he did come, I remember I was like maybe two years old, and we lived downtown because they managed an apartment. Then we moved to Imperial Highway and then eventually we settled on 78th Street and San Pedro when I was three years old. And my family lived there for sixty-one years until my mother died in 2014.

When my grandfather, my mother's father, died back in Louisiana, my mom sent him a shirt to be buried in and that was it. She didn't go to the funeral. She never went to funerals anyway, but why didn't she go to her own father's funeral? He left her property, but she never went back to claim it. I don't know what happened between them, where the animosity came from, but obviously there was something. I always figured it was molestation or something like that. It had to be something deep for her to feel like that.

My mom came from Louisiana with this preconceived notion of being better because we were Catholic and from Louisiana. She always told us we were better. She kept us from certain kids. We couldn't play with what she called "pickaninnies." But I had to go to school with these same kids that she had been calling out of their name. My mom never used the word "Creole" to describe us even though I suspect that's how she thought and felt about us. But she never said it out loud because of my dad. He didn't put up with that, but it wouldn't have worked for me anyway because I knew better at a young age.

Neither of my parents were religious. Being from Louisiana, my mom was raised Catholic, but she wasn't fervent about it. She sent me and my sisters to Mother of Sorrows on 87th and Main because it was closest to our house, but when we were kicked out of there because I didn't understand all the rituals and wouldn't participate, she didn't stress about it much. When it came time for the communion I wouldn't come forward. I didn't understand what the priest was talking about. So, I asked him one Sunday: "You said this was the body of Christ, but if he has no eyes or legs, how is this the body?" Between that, and my sister Valerie kicking the Mother Superior, we were out of there.

When I was a child, we had a couple of pets: Fluffy, a miniature Collie, and Tom, a tomcat. For some reason, my mom didn't like female animals, and she also didn't like little dogs. We kept pigeons, and later my mom kept German shepherds. She always wanted something that could "take care of business" and "protect the house." We never kept any extra puppies or kittens. We had no hamsters— they looked too much like mice—but we did have some goldfish. Fluffy and Tom were cool, though. Tom used to attack dogs. He'd wait in a tree, then jump on them.

I am the oldest of my parents' three daughters. My middle sister, Valerie Sue, was born in 1954. Valerie was once the homecoming queen of Fremont High, and she was a mathematical genius who understood calculus when she was fourteen. She had been admitted into a university well before she graduated from high school. She got an after-school job at Security Pacific Bank, and they eventually placed her with the manager because she was so smart. She almost took his job, and she was only seventeen at the time.

We found out years later that Valerie was bipolar with schizophrenia. Of course, we didn't know what it was called back then. Mathematics is a whole different language, and that's how her mind worked because she was very abstract. She married Chester Lemon, who went to Fremont with us. Chester would go on to play for the Chicago White Sox and the Detroit Tigers baseball teams. Baseball is how they met; Valerie was the statistician for the boys' varsity team.

My youngest sister, Felicia Elaine, who was born in 1957, married Chester's brother Edward. Both Valerie and Felicia ended up having four children. Felicia was also brilliant, but she too would later be diagnosed with mental illness. Unfortunately, her mental illness prevented her from doing a lot of things. I had always felt there was something off about my sisters, but I loved them and that's the only thing I knew. I adored them and protected them, and we all got along as children and teenagers.

I was the type that would go and experience the things of the world, whereas my sisters would not. I would call myself adventurous. Once I became an avowed nationalist, none of them understood it, so I was sort of isolated from my sisters while the two of them remained very close to one another. I think my sisters and my parents were all afraid for me once I made the decision to join a political nationalist organization. For me, I saw it as a natural progression.

All throughout elementary school I had to fight. It was always one thing or another. Girls would come at me because I had real long hair and they wanted to cut it. Or they'd tell me "You know, your sister is high yella," or something like that because one of my sisters is fair, lighter than me. Or they'd say, "Your daddy is a white man." My dad was Seminole, Cuban, and African. He considered himself Black and he was proud of that. But everybody thought he was a white man. They really didn't know what he was. I have a picture of him among a whole bunch of Latinos and you can't distinguish him from any of them. So, you know he got away with quite a bit. If he had actually been seen as a Black man, it probably would have been a lot harder on him.

I went to 75th Street Elementary and Edison Junior High Schools. I was an A student, but I also wouldn't "cooperate." That's what one of my teachers wrote on my report card, that I've always been a rebel. Sometimes the teachers bored me because I thought some of them were pretty slow. I had been reading so much I was bored easily, and I would be what you call today a "problem child." But I also played violin; I was trained in the flute, I did ballet and tap, and I was a narrator at all of the plays that happened in elementary school.

Back then, 75th Street and Edison were all-Black schools because the whole community was Black. This was before busing, where Black children had to get up early, sometimes before dawn, and then travel by bus into the San Fernando Valley, or wherever the whites had fled to, and went to their schools. There was no reverse busing of white kids into Fremont or Manual Arts. Once the whites left, they stayed gone. We went to the schools in our immediate neighborhood. There was one white girl at 75th Street School named Anna Dunlap. I'll never forget her because she spit on me one day after school and I ran and caught her in her house.

I didn't trust many people when I was in elementary school, and I stayed that way through high school, the Us Organization, and even now. I was a loner, and I chose my friends very, very carefully. I was close to the twins Claude and Claudette McGarrety when I was at 75th Street. Their parents owned a café in the neighborhood. I had one good friend, Deborah Tate, and our friendship lasted from elementary school all the way to college.

A lot of my teachers had a problem with me, but not all of them. There was Mr. Brown, who was my homeroom teacher. I remember him because he once said to me, "You know what, De-BOR-ah?" He was the first one to correctly pronounce my name. He said, "De-BOR-ah, you're going to have problems, so get ready. Get ready for the battle."

"You stand out as different," he said. "You are very well educated but you're educated in more things than one. There's also something worldly about you. Even at this age, there's something a little bit deeper about you than you are now." He always encouraged me to stand for my individuality but not to be such a know-it-all. This was when I was in the fifth grade.

I was reading things that piqued my interest, so that put me on a whole different thought process, even in listening to music. Of course I liked ANYTHING from Motown, who didn't?! But I also liked Olatunji, the Nigerian drummer, and Miriam Makeba, the South African singer. Their music would sometimes be playing at Ken's house when I would be there with all the other kids, but so would jazz and R&B, which is what my mom loved.

Since my dad was an intellectual, when we came home from school we were still in school. We read dictionaries like Malcolm did. We read encyclopedias, all kinds of books. It was constant learning. We went to museums and my dad would explain the different artists. It was my father who turned me on to James Baldwin and Langston Hughes at that young age, and most of my schoolmates weren't reading any of that then.

Ours was an unconventional childhood in the 1950s. We were introduced to so many things that a lot of other kids in South Central Los Angeles, kids our age, didn't experience, like riding horses, fishing, camping at Yosemite, and going to Yellowstone and the Grand Canyon.

We never felt the pressure of discrimination here in Los Angeles. My first recollection of that was when we went to Disneyland when it first opened; we were one of the first Black people to enter and they would hardly even let Black people in back then.

When Disneyland first started out, it was among orange groves; it's not the Disneyland of today. And I think that was in 1955, so I must have been five when we first went. And these people looked at us, these little Black kids and my dad, and they're thinking he's a white man. They looked and you could tell the looks, even then. I look back now and I can remember those looks. So, that's when we knew something was going on in the world. We would go places and get looks. We went horseback riding with Charles Bronson's kids. We were taught to ski, we were taught to swim, there was no limit.

I started reading at the age of three, so I was always up on things.

I didn't even call myself an American at that young age. I've always considered myself African, not Black. I was never confused.

I never wanted to vote because I knew the game. This is how I had been long before I first met Ken when I was nine. As far as cliques were concerned, I never was involved in any of that. I knew I was different. I liked being different; some people would call it peculiar. This is where my mother and I clashed because my mom wanted me to be in the social scene, a debutante and all that. She would say, "Well, you're going to be a congresswoman one day and we've already got the plan for you." And I can remember just looking at her and thinking, "If you only knew . . . you're sitting across from a stranger." She really didn't know me at all.

When I met Ken, he was fourteen. In his late teens he got married, and he and his wife moved down the street but not too far from his parents. By that time Ken had changed his name to Msemaji, Kiswahili for "Orator." He and his wife identified themselves as nationalists. They were among a heavy presence of people with ideas and aims in the neighborhood. There were the Red Guards. They were Maoists who had also set up shop in the neighborhood across the street from Fremont High School. I was young when I first met them, but they gave me Mao's Red Book. Because of my age I was thinking, "This has nothing to do with us, this is Chinese."

But I ended up studying with the Red Guards. I studied with Msemaji and folks. Just like when he was a kid, Msemaji still had people coming to his house to read books and discuss information and news about what was happening to Black people. I also met Bird when I was young. Bird was a tall and heavyset kid who went to Fremont (when he decided he would go to class), and he used to hang out in front of my apartment building with some of his friends. Bird and his friends all eventually became the founders of the Slausons, one of the largest and most well-known Black gangs in Los Angeles.

It was through Bird that I met Bunchy Carter. Back then the neighborhood-based gangs came about as Black folks began to move into the previously white areas, West of Central Avenue and South into Watts. White youths who called themselves "spook hunters" and would terrorize Black youths as their parents were trying to hold on to their little enclaves. Eventually, white flight won out and whites fled South Central Los Angeles and the surrounding areas. People today are surprised when they hear that Compton used to be all white!

Lots of the gang members that joined for community protection would eventually join the Black Power Movement. Once the movement had been defeated by COINTELPRO and internal contradictions, a new generation of gang members turned on the community they had once protected.

When the Panthers came along, I studied with them also because I had friends who had joined them. Even though I was very politically aware, I wasn't on the "political" kick. I was more of the African or Pan-African kick. That's why later, an organization like Us, appealed to me. I liked the Panthers because a lot of my friends were Panthers, but I was African. I knew even as a kid that I was African and a nationalist. It was just natural for me, though it wasn't natural in my family. My mother was totally against me getting involved in anything political. She never wavered from that.

Growing up across the street from Fremont High, a lot of us came from the same neighborhood. Names that people read in history books today, a lot of us knew as kids. We grew up together and went to school together. Some of those guys who became Slausons used to sit on our porch. Our apartment faced the front gates of the school, so the guys would cross the street to go home but they'd stop and hangout and just sit on the porch or mess around play fighting on the lawn or hiding around the bush or the tree. They weren't ditching school; they were just hanging out. The duplex had these steps and a big open porch area. At the time, I didn't go to Fremont with them because they were older than me, but they used to sit out on the porch because it was convenient, and sometimes we'd talk.

My mother thought differently. At the time, my mother was thinking, "Here's these older guys and I've got three daughters? Nope." She would sometimes go outside and start sweeping the porch or turn on the water hose to water the bushes and the flowers. She'd miss the bushes and the flowers and wet up the porch and whoever was sitting there instead. Sometimes she'd mention out loud that she kept a gun in the house as she was sweeping.

But that's how I met a lot of them. I'd come outside and they'd be sitting there: Lafayette, Skillet, Bird. They weren't hurting anyone or anything. They protected me like big brothers. Bird always said he admired me even as a kid. We all knew one another and hung together. We all lived in the same all-Black community. These were hard-working people who had homes and paid mortgages. We didn't judge people arbitrarily. Just because someone was a Slauson didn't mean they weren't a good person. As long as one person treated another with respect, everything was fine.

That was pretty much the attitude in the community back then.

3

GIRL/HOOD

CRUNCH! CRUNCH! CRUNCH!
Ugh, God! Come on, Mom!

When I was a girl, my mom would put starch in the slips we would wear under our dresses and skirts. It was just about *the* most embarrassing thing ever. I was a skinny kid so the dress would make me look like I was an umbrella. When I sat down the starch would make all this noise because of all the stiffness. I would be sitting in class trying to be completely still, not moving at all. It was awful.

During the 1950s and '60s little girls would dress up in frilly clothes. We would look . . . "girly." It fit in perfectly with my mom's position that "a child is seen and not heard." I'm from that generation; when it came to my clothing, style of dress, or too many "outside" influences like the TV, there was no discussion to be had. So, the style of clothing of that time is what I wore. The typical dresses that girls used to wear—whether it was to play hopscotch, jump rope, or fight—would be in those exact same dresses. We didn't wear pants and tennis shoes and stuff like that to school. We didn't have a bunch of "play clothes." We had clothes for Sunday School, maybe one or two dresses for the girls, one suit for the boys (our "good clothes"), and the rest of our clothing was for school. But we dressed as nicely and as "frilly" as our parents could afford. I didn't enjoy being in those dresses but there was nothing I could do.

I started Edison Junior High School in 1962 when I turned twelve. The school was on the East side, at 65th Street and Hooper Avenue, between Florence and Gage Avenues and one block east of Central Avenue. There was no busing during this time, taking Black kids into white areas. Edison, like Fremont and a few other schools, was all Black.

We would walk to Edison in groups. We'd leave about 7 a.m. and meet up with other kids along the way, and we'd make it to campus with plenty of time before school started at 8 a.m. When school let out around 3 p.m., we'd meet up again and walk home. Most of the student body came from the surrounding neighborhood. One or two kids took public transportation, and a couple had parents who dropped them off or picked them up, but for the majority of us, we walked to and from school since we lived in the area.

I would usually come straight home during those Edison days. I didn't really participate in school extracurricular activities until high school. I would do my homework from school and then the homework my parents gave me, reading from the encyclopedia or the dictionary. Like I said before, we did a lot of traveling as a family and it was a lot of fun, but it was also educational.

As far as extracurriculars I did a lot of things that weren't tied to Edison. I was in the Girl Scouts, and I also had ballet, tap, music, and other dance classes that my parents paid for. I took flute and violin lessons and public speaking. My mom was preparing me for a world that I really had no interest in joining: becoming a good American citizen. Looking back, I shouldn't have complained so much. For all intents and purposes my childhood ended when I was twelve. That was when my father went to prison.

My father was sent to San Quentin for eight years in 1962. At the time, I didn't know where he was. My mother didn't want us to know he was in prison. She cooked up a story for us at the time, and between his phone calls home and his letters, it wasn't until I was seventeen that our neighbor, Sandra Branche, told me that he was in prison. I didn't believe her; but what she'd said was true. He was in San Quentin for distributing marijuana.

My mom had a dilemma on her hands: my father had been our sole provider and my mother had been a homemaker. Now, my mother needed to work but she didn't really know how since she had been taken care of by my father. But when she did start working, she didn't stop. She worked for forty-something years, almost until she died. But at the moment, when my father went away, we were temporarily lost. So, I took it upon myself to help take care of my sisters and my mother. I called myself stepping up to the plate.

My mom couldn't cope without her husband, and we had been in escrow on a five-bedroom home when my dad went to prison. So, we ended up losing that. It was a traumatic time for all of us and my mother was in total turmoil. I did my part to help by getting my sisters together for school. I made breakfast and lunch, washed and laid out the school clothes. After school, I came home and did my homework, helped make dinner, and made sure my mother was okay. The situation put a tremendous strain on her, so much so that she came under a doctor's care, and he began to give her Valium shots. I didn't like her being on those shots, so I never liked that doctor for giving them to her. I hated the days she would have a doctor's appointment. She would leave the house okay, but once she came home she would just be out of it.

My father had been the backbone and now that was missing. I figured I had to be the backbone now because I was the oldest. But I was a child dealing with two younger sisters, little kids that I was now responsible for, and I also had to be there for my mom. I just got tired because it was all so much, so I started running away. I didn't think of it as running away at the time, however. I thought of it as more of a "staying away." I didn't want to go home.

At one point while my father was away my mother had a boyfriend. I never liked him, and I told him so. He would try to tell me what to do, and not only would I tell him he wasn't my daddy, but I also told him my daddy would be coming back. I didn't really want to be around when he was there, so I would stay over at somebody's house. Sometimes I'd stay at the Seatons' on their couch, or at other children's homes. The parents would let me stay a night or two, but I'd eventually have to leave. They weren't kicking me out per se; they were just of the opinion that a twelve-year-old child should be home with her own parents and siblings. But there were lots of times when I'd stay at school or the library and do my schoolwork for as long as I could stay. Sometimes I would do my homework on the couches in other people's living rooms. A lot of those nights became last-minute sleepovers. I was the only one who knew the truth. And all the while I never missed school and I graduated on time.

But I started "running" away and that was a cause of concern for my mom. Back then, if you ran away, they sent you to juvenile hall. It was standard practice for kids who were considered runaways. And that's what happened to me. My best friend at the time, Debra Tate, was concerned about me as well as my mom, so the both of them got together and called the police. You can imagine how shocked I was! My mom gave them permission to take me to juvenile hall as a runaway because her thinking was, "Well, I'll know where you are now. I don't have to wonder whether or not you're dead or what's going on with you. This way I can reach out and touch." The police picked me up and handcuffed me like I had committed some criminal act. *What is happening here?! What's going on?!* I thought to myself. I was thirteen that first time I was sent off to MacLaren Hall.

MacLaren Hall was this huge place in El Monte, about twenty miles or so past Boyle Heights in East Los Angeles. It took up ten acres of land. It wasn't originally built for juvenile delinquents; it was actually intended to be a place for "unfortunate" children: those who were abused, neglected, unwanted, abandoned, or orphaned. It was actually built to house the children who weren't considered delinquent, but that soon changed. MacLaren was a "kid's prison." It even had razor wire and those big spotlights like they have in adult prison. But just like in adult prison, kids would escape from MacLaren Hall too.

One side of MacLaren Hall was all girls and the other side was all boys. Back then, the boys at MacLaren Hall would pick up everyone's laundry and the girls would do all the washing. That was the mentality in society at large and the same mentality at MacLaren Hall. The girls always did the laundry, ironing, indoor work, all that kind of stuff. Boys would do heavy lifting and yard or outside work. I never fit into the girls' mode, however. I stayed in solitary confinement.

Being in juvenile hall was a very traumatic experience for me. When they place you in there, you don't know at the time that these other kids, most of whom are older, have committed some heavy crimes no different than the adults, including murder. They just happened to be teenagers. I had never been around kids that stole, lied, and cheated. A couple had even killed their own parents! That's what was there at MacLaren Hall. I had to get a different type of mentality in order to protect myself.

The housing at MacLaren Hall was like a college dormitory, but this was far from a college. Other girls always wanted to fight. There were lesbians who wanted to turn you out. There were those who were struggling for power. Bullies who just wanted to rule over you and take what you had. If your parents sent you something they'd take it and that was that. It was no different than any jail. It was the same thing, only these were kids and not adults.

There was no relationship to speak of with the counselors there. That's not why you were there. In juvenile hall, it's like a mini prison. They were not out to help you or to rehabilitate you or anything like that. There were no social workers.

My first day at MacLaren some girls tried to jump me, but it didn't work. They were talking about "turning me out." I was able to get to the leader of these girls and that squashed that. I was threatened every single day. They sharpened their pencils, or they'd take a toothbrush and they'd make it into some kind of little weapon and hide it underneath their clothes. So, I did too. It was a prison-jail mentality and it's all about survival. I had to learn that even if I was fighting for my life and defending myself, that I would be the likely one put into solitary confinement. I stayed in solitary confinement for six months out of the twelve months I was there the first time.

The reason I ended up staying a year is because my mom wouldn't let me come home. When they take you to court to determine what will happen to you, they ask your parent, "Do you want her to come home?" My mother said, "No," so I had to go back. There was no other place to put me.

My mother may have done this because, in her mind, it was out of love and caring, but I never really got what her mindset was. I never asked her because I was so angry with her for sending me there.

I was sent to MacLaren again when I was fifteen for the same thing, running away from home. Once again, my mom's thinking was, "Well, the streets are a cold-blooded place for a kid, but juvenile hall was safer for her." Which was sort of true. There were evil adults out there in those streets then just like it is right now. Grown-ups tried to rape me and do a lot of things to me when I was a teen.

Once when I was fifteen, before I had been sent off to MacLaren that second time, I was walking down San Pedro with a group of other teens from school. We had just gotten out of class for the day and we were going to hang out at this food spot when a car with three men drove up. We weren't walking in a tight group; we were spread out and I was in the rear of the group. One of the guys got out of the car and pulled a gun on me. He pressed it into my back and pushed me toward the car. I was basically kidnapped in broad daylight to be put on "the block"—work as a prostitute—in Long Beach. The things they said to me, the plans they had, and what they wanted to do scared me.

I was scared, but I didn't panic. Back in the day, everybody carried knives. This wasn't a gang thing or anything; adults and kids carried knives like they carried pens. They were simply tools you kept on you. And yes, some of us girls carried knives too. My father is the one who gave me my knife. Crime wasn't out of control, but you also didn't want to "get caught slipping," as the young people say! "Better to have it and not need it, than to need it and not have it." Carrying knives was just something people did.

I was wearing some cute, girly boots that came up my calves and my knife was in there. I was scared, but I kept my hands on my knees so I could get to the knife quickly. We stopped at a liquor store and two of the guys got out. The third guy, who was driving, started telling me how "it" was going to happen to me: how all three were going to "break me in." He kept on talking but he turned his head for a moment and that's when I made my move, striking like a snake: I went into my boot, pulled my knife out and put it right to his neck. I stuck the tip of the blade in his neck, and I'm not really sure why, but I told him to give me his wallet, then I scrambled out of the back seat and ran as fast as I could down the street. I was on the track team during my junior year at Fremont . . . That's how fast I could run. I was running for my life. I flagged down a cab, came right back to Fremont, paid the driver with that guy's money, and walked home. I never told anyone about that. I went right back to school the next day. It's something how the brain works and puts bad things to the back so you can "carry on!"

"Carry on" is exactly what I did. My teenage love at that time was a boy named Nathaniel Clark. He was a year older than me. Tall, lanky, and light-brown skin; he had a very gentle smile. He was always sweet to me. He would hold my hand and put his arm around my shoulder; not like he owned me, more like he was protecting me. He would later become a Black Panther. Something happened to Nathaniel after he became a Panther, but I never heard exactly what it was that happened to him. I know that he was harassed, beaten, and arrested by the police several times. Whatever happened to him changed him. He was shot and killed by his wife in September of 1968. She said he had been very violent toward her during their entire marriage and she couldn't take it anymore. He had never been violent towards me, however. I was saddened to learn of his passing that way: not at the hands of the police, but by a woman he was supposed to have loved. He was nineteen years old.

It's always easier to strike at those closest to you even though they are not your real enemy.

The majority of people I knew when I was going to Fremont would go on to join the Panthers except my best friend Debra Tate. She was always one of the most intelligent people I knew since elementary school. She always had my back and was always trying to steer me in the right direction. Which is why she joined with my mom in calling the cops on me. She actually thought she was helping me!

In those days, those were the choices that were available for a kid like me: the streets or juvenile hall. My mother thought I was in good hands, but meanwhile, my reality in juvenile hall was that the girls there were doing some of the same things the adults out on the streets were doing.

And I still went to school while all that madness was taking place. MacLaren had a so-called school that really didn't help. I was able to graduate from Fremont on time because I always had taken extra credits. So even though I had missed an entire year at Fremont, and the school at MacLaren was a joke, I was ahead of the game. I half-heartedly attended classes at MacLaren because they weren't teaching me anything; it was just part of the routine.

I was an A student when I was at Fremont. School had never been a problem for me. I just found it boring because I was a big reader, so I was ahead of most of the students, and I wanted to discuss things outside of the standard curriculum. Once I came home after being in MacLaren for one year, I went back to school just like a regular student, but now I'm in total rebellion because I'm angry at my mom, I'm angry at the system, I'm angry at the streets. I'm angry because my dad is nowhere to be found. I'm just angry at everybody. And so, I rebelled even more.

I smoked my first joint and drank my first beer: Old English. I was rebellious, but . . . I wasn't that rebellious. I wasn't into sex like a lot of young rebelling girls my age were. My thing was that a boy was a friend and he did what I told him to do. That was my definition of having a boyfriend! I don't know, maybe it was because my mother had drilled it into our heads so much that having sex at that age was nothing to be proud of and nothing to aspire to. She would say, "My girls are beautiful and brilliant. Do not think what is between your legs is the bank. It is stupid to call your vagina the pocketbook." She would get in our faces, take her finger, and point to my (or whichever one of us she was talking to) forehead and say, "This is the bank. Use it well."

All that drilling into my head must've paid off because I didn't lose my virginity while I was in high school. A lot of other girls did. My best friend Debra lost her virginity, but not me. Debra had started having sex when we were at Edison. She was about fourteen then. She never got pregnant though. My friend Claudette was also having sex. She liked older guys, probably because she was a little bit older than us. Girls would talk about the boys they liked, and if a girl was having sex, it would come out that way. We didn't talk about contraceptives (which would've been hard to come by). And the only time we would really know if a girl was pregnant was if she was wearing a coat during the summer. I was so naïve about sex and sexuality at that age!

Once, my friend Debra took me to a party at someone's house. I didn't know the person, but she did. She really wanted me to go, so I went with her, and when we got there she wanted me to dance with some boys. "He's cute, dance with him," or, "See that guy over there? He's looking at you, you should dance with him." I couldn't tell how she knew who was cute and who was ugly since a red light bulb had been screwed into the socket and it was dark in there. My eyes eventually adjusted to the darkness and there was a slow song playing. Everybody was "grinding" on each other at the party! I didn't know about that sort of thing. I didn't do that. I never did that.

Another time, I had gone into the girls' bathroom at Fremont, and as I entered the stall I heard some girls near the window talking about Claudette. They were saying that she sucked dick and they called her a whore. I finished what I was doing and came out of the stall and asked which one of them was saying those things about Claudette. The girl spoke up and I started whaling on her. Even though Claudette was older than me she was my friend, and I was loyal to my friends. I said to myself, *You're not going to be talking bad about somebody I've known since the age of three.* I wasn't having it.

So, of course, I wound up in the principal's office. Mr. Redmond was a tall, slender white man with a head full of salt-and-pepper, hair and he wore thin, gold-wire rimmed glasses. When he was serious, he'd lower his head slightly and look over the top of them, his thin nose pointing directly at you. He asked me what was going on. I told him, "These girls were saying my friend sucked dick." Then I said, "See Jane run, run Dick run," and he didn't like that. He turned red as a stop sign.

A lot of people assumed I was "fast" because I knew a lot of boys. I wasn't "fast." That's not what it was. I was a tomboy when I was coming up, despite my "girly" attire. I was good at athletics, like track. I really didn't know anything about sex, oral or otherwise, when I was in high school. "See Dick run" was the extent of my knowledge about "dicks."

Even though I sometimes hung around boys, they were always more interested in me than I was in them. There were several times I had to literally run to get away from them. Boys would hit on me, and I would tell them I wasn't interested, and they wouldn't leave me alone. They wouldn't take no for an answer. A couple of times, boys would chase me, and I would run home, but I wouldn't run in the house. I would run through the alley and hide in our garage, and when the boys got there, I would hit them with a piece of wood. Not a stick, but a two by four: a two-foot by four-foot piece of wood. Ernest Luther, Michael Ford, and Freddy Jones were some of the boys who found out the hard way that I wasn't interested in them. By them pursuing me like that, that would be considered sexual harassment today. I didn't think they were really going to harm me, but I didn't like them trying to force me to be with them. I didn't like them trying to make me do something I didn't want to do. So, they found out the hard and painful way.

I've always been this way. I just naturally resist anyone who tries to force me to do something.

I didn't have a sex problem when I was in high school, but that was my first introduction to drugs and alcohol. We would eventually have a long-term relationship.

When I got out of MacLaren I entered the tenth grade and breezed through, while still mad at my mom and rebelling, and still reading and thinking and growing. I was really calling myself an African nationalist now. I was reading about Nelson Mandela, who had been imprisoned for life on South Africa's Robben Island. Mandela had been a lawyer who'd joined the anti-apartheid struggle with his good friend Walter Sisulu. They were convicted of sabotage for blowing up buildings in the struggle to end the brutal and savage white minority government. That was when Mandela gave his famous speech about being prepared to die to wage the struggle to free South Africa.

I was reading about the struggles in Africa and the Caribbean, and of course the civil rights battles right here in the US were still happening. I was consuming all this information. But at that same time, my mom was going through her own struggles of being a single mom for the first time and having to go to work. She needed support because her husband was imprisoned. It really took its toll on my mom. My parents didn't divorce during this time. I loved my dad, but even at that age I thought that if my mom had left my dad, maybe it might have brought some peace. Folks didn't really do that then—get divorced because of imprisonment. I think a divorce would have brought some peace, and that's what I was searching for. I never found peace during that time period, no matter how hard or where I looked. So, I just kind of went with the flow of things.

What else could I do?

My running away continued, so it was off to MacLaren Hall for that second time when I was fifteen. Was this becoming a cycle? No different than when criminals go back in and then come out grown adults? It was the same type of mentality, even for the teenager. I can't explain the psychology of it. I was just really angry. I was angry and I had no one to turn to or talk to. This time I only stayed in MacLaren for six months. I came home and, once again, didn't miss a beat and went straight into the eleventh grade. One more year and I would graduate from high school.

In 1968, I was headed towards my eighteenth birthday, but I was still having problems at home. I was older but not grown yet and still under the rule of my mom. This time, instead of juvenile hall, my mom sent me to live with a family we had known for several years. She called it putting me in a "safe environment" with her friends Eva, my godmother, and her husband Harvey. That too didn't last long once Harvey tried to assault me.

Since I was a kid, I had been around a lot of folks who would eventually become Panthers. I was nine years old when I was around Ken, who became Msemaji and joined Us. Now I'm a teenager and there was a movement going on and I wanted to join it. My mom was concerned, but at this time she wasn't worried about me running away. She's worried about this political-nationalist movement stuff. I wanted to be that type of nationalist and my mother didn't understand anything about that. She was pro-American: red, white, and blue. My mom thought that putting me with Eva and Harvey, who seemed to be a stable couple, would perhaps keep me safe from both the streets and "wild-eyed nationalists." My mom thought she was putting me in a different environment. Juvenile hall didn't work, so maybe Eva and Harvey would straighten me out.

Eva was Catholic and kept an altar in the home with all this light and Madonna stuff she would worship. She was a good woman. But her husband was another story. One afternoon I was in the house alone, or so I thought. I was in my room on the bed napping when Harvey came in. I didn't hear a knock or my name called. I was startled awake, and when I looked at him, he asked me what I was doing. I could tell he wasn't really interested in my answer. He was wearing an undershirt and in his boxer underwear. This grown, married man was in the room with me in his underwear, and my godmother was nowhere to be found. Harvey stood a foot away from the bed and smiled at me. I looked him in the eye, then glanced over to the window that was open. I guess he figured out that I was thinking about an escape route because that's when he lunged at me. Before he could grab me, I kicked my foot out and it met his face. I rolled off the side of the bed and dove out the window. Fortunately, it was only a one-story house. I ran for my life to a friend's house a few blocks away. I stayed there for a few days, refusing to come back to my mom's house. I never told her or Eva about what Harvey had done. I just let my mom assume I was doing my usual runaway routine, but that was the next-to-last incident I endured before I made the decision to join the Us Organization. After I left Eva and Harvey's house I joined almost immediately. Almost. I had a detour first.

One night after I had run away from Eva and Harvey's house, I was hanging out with some people not far from Fremont. The Panthers had an office right down the street from the school and a bunch of us kids and a few Panthers were outside. The police rolled up and made everyone put their hands up. All us kids in the group kept our mouths shut but the Panthers gave the cops pure hell. Before I knew it, more cars rolled up and all of us were taken to jail. Every last one of us was carted off. Once we got to the county jail, they booked the men in and separated all the females. A small contingent of youths were sent to MacLaren Hall. I thought to myself, *Oh God, here I go again to this place!* but I was wrong. I was put on the bus with some older women and sent to the Sybil Brand Institute for Women!

I was seventeen years old and I should have been sent to juvenile hall! I was nervous and scared because the cops had been harassing a lot of my friends who were politically active. My friends told us the stories. I thought, *I'm not even active, I wasn't even doing anything!* But I also remembered something my mother would say to me: "Never let the world see you cry. Never let the world see you sweat." I wanted to cry so badly, but my mom's words in my head wouldn't let me.

Sybil Brand had been built for women in 1963 and named for this woman who was an advocate for women prisoners. Before Sybil Brand was built, women were held in the jail at the LA County Courthouse. I told myself to buckle up because I was going to where the real deal existed.

Thieves, prostitutes, lifers, and murderers; they were all present and accounted for at Sybil Brand. I remember when they brought us in that night, the women were being separated from the main population. Some of them looked so manly I thought they were actually men. The women there called it the "daddy tank." The prostitutes would take off their wigs and go be with those women. I immediately saw that I had a decision to make. I wasn't going to be a follower of any one and I couldn't afford to be weak. "Only the strong survive," my mother used to always say.

I was processed in and assigned a cell on the fourth floor. My cellmate was a white girl from Long Beach named Janice. Janice was a little older than me and had been there a couple of weeks. She had been arrested for shoplifting. We got along pretty good together. The routine when you were in Brand was that they woke you up every morning at 5 a.m. The cell had a toilet, a sink, and a bunk bed for two people. You would stand ready for them to open the cell doors and you step out. They call you by the number you're given when they process you. Then they line you up for roll call and give you a lousy breakfast and you better hope you don't have an enemy in the kitchen. Once I saw a woman convulsing and screaming and spitting up blood. The word was that someone had put finely ground glass in her food. They took her off to the infirmary, but I didn't hear what became of her. After eating breakfast, you go back to your cell for hours, out for lunch, back to your cell, then out again for dinner. Everything is routine.

There's work for everyone at Brand: kitchen, laundry, cleaning showers, as well as keeping yourself clean. The Honor Group was where you worked with the guards, known as trustees today. The guards were in jail right along with us. They would have their favorites and they would provide drugs, certain foods, or even clothes, such as new underwear, to the women of their choosing.

I would listen to these women's stories about how they wound up in there, and what would amaze me most of the time was that their stories all dealt with men. I also noticed that they didn't receive the same support as men in jail would. But I remained silent, listening and learning. Many of the women there were repeat offenders. Many of them had been in jail more than fifteen times.

Of course, women can be very vicious, just like the men. There were lots of fights over all sorts of things. There were cliques and alliances, and you had to know who was who and what they were into. I wasn't into cliques and I wasn't going to join one now. I had never been into them, not even in high school. I decided to keep my mouth shut and learn the system. There was a group of women who appeared to be running the section I was staying in. They told all the other women what to do and they took what they wanted. They also raped other women. As I said, the women could be just as vicious as the men. After a while this group of women that were running things focused on Janice and me.

The day finally arrived when they came into our cell. I was among the youngest of the inmates at Brand, and my cellmate Janice was about two years older than me. Instead of being in juvenile hall, here I was in Brand with these real-deal criminals. The real-dealers decided to attack Janice on this day. For some reason, there were no guards around and I witnessed what the true horror of jail life could be. These women beat Janice badly, took a broom handle and stuck it up her rectum, then they all took turns raping her with that same broom handle and beating her. I wanted to jump in and help her, but the first thing they said to me was to stay out of it. They told Janice the next time she received money for commissary, they would collect it. She became their slave.

I figured I must be next since I was so young, so I told Janice that she would have to now sleep on the bottom bunk. I decided that when they came into the cell for me, I'd leap from the top bunk and thus be in a better position to fight for my life. I wasn't going to be anybody's slave.

The day came when the group came back and of course, again, there were no guards around. Once they got inside the cell, I leapt off the top bunk and went straight for the leader, a young Mexican woman named Anita. I think she was in her early twenties, and I had heard she was being held on an assault charge. I flew off that bunk and went straight for Anita's head. I grabbed her and swung her by her long black hair onto the floor of the cell and began punching her in the face. I rained down punches and kicks on her head and body. Although her followers were hitting me, I paid them no mind, my priority was Anita. I was trying to kill her. I had her where she was about to give up. She kept yelling for me to let her go. I'd say to her, "Call your dog's off me!" She wouldn't do it and I'd go right back to raining down punches and kicks. We made enough noise that a couple of guards finally appeared, and they took Anita, me, and all the other women in front of a sergeant, a couple of administrators, and the director of the place.

As soon as we went before them, they started asking questions to find out what happened. It was supposed to be a trial; in actuality, it was a mockery. What surprised me most was that I was the one accused of being the problem! They asked me if I would do it again. Here I was, defending myself, preventing myself from being raped and whatever else those women had planned for me, and here were the authorities, agreeing with this foul behavior. And they had the nerve to ask me would I do it again? Would I defend myself? "HELL YES!" I yelled at them. "You all wanted this to happen! You're ALL lesbians!" I tossed in. *That* little outburst sealed my fate. The guards at Brand were white and female, just like the ones at MacLaren. Next thing I knew, they were taking me under the jail.

I was sent to solitary confinement, deep in the bowels of Sybil Brand. A guard walked a few paces behind me as we walked down a long, dark corridor. I heard screaming and cussing and there was the foulest odor I had ever smelled. It was beyond filthy. The guard escorting me said this was where they kept the criminally insane. So that's where they put me. It wasn't really solitary confinement because there was another woman in the cell with me, but it was still hell.

In the regular cells, up above where human civilization dwelled, the doors opened by an automatic switch. Down there in hell, they opened the doors to the cells with a large, old-fashioned key. They opened a door at the very end of the corridor and pushed me in. There were no windows and there was no bunk bed. There was a steel toilet, and standing in the corner was a huge, filthy white woman, with nails on her hands so long they looked like claws. She looked right at me and said, "I'm a sadist." By this time any fear I had since first coming to Brand had been replaced with nothing but rage. I met her stare with my own and told her in the coldest voice I could muster, "So am I... Wwhat we need is a masochist... because if you try anything I'll kill your ass."

I had no trouble with her.

I was confined beneath the jail with no work assignment. All I had was time to sit and think, so that's what I did. A myriad of thoughts went through my head. I thought of being in juvenile hall and now adult jail. I thought about the pimps that tried to kidnap me and life on the streets as a runaway. I thought of my mom placing me with a family that we knew and trusted because she thought it was safe for me, yet the father attempted to rape me. I thought about all these things as I was in a cell with a criminally insane person who scratched her body, ate her own feces, and played in her period blood. I remember thinking I had reached the sixth circle of hell. Or was it the seventh?

Every night there would be screams from the other women that would go on and on. My cellmate, her name escapes me now, would scream and howl in the beginning. At first I would threaten to beat the hell out of her if she didn't stay quiet. Truth be told, I had only intended on scaring her. I was only going to harm her if she harmed me. I would threaten to beat her ass once she started screaming, then she'd remember and be quiet. I grew tired of threatening her and decided I'd try to quiet her with food. The food was awful. It really shouldn't have been called food and I couldn't bring myself to eat it. But I pretended it was wonderful and I would bribe her: "If you don't yell or scream at all tonight, I'll give you my breakfast in the morning." For a while that ended up working much better than my threats.

The "food" in solitary was served in duty dishes—thick trays with sections for each piece of slop they served you—and three glasses of water in the morning, at noon, and at night. I had heard that the prison put "saltpeter"—a mineral called potassium nitrate—in the food to curb the women's sexual urges. I found out years later that was a myth, but you could tell it wasn't true by just looking around you. Consensual relationships and rape were the norm. Women didn't even get punished for having sex despite what the rules said. The only time a woman was punished for having sex was when she refused to engage in a sexual act or committed some other transgression, like I did.

There were no clocks down where I was and the guards wouldn't talk to you and tell you the time, so you could only assume the time. This little routine went on for a few weeks. Eventually they threw another woman in the cell with us. This one would use her feces to write on the walls.

A person couldn't imagine a life like that. You couldn't fathom your mind and body constantly going through such an ordeal. I was confined underneath Sybil Brand for nine months. During this time my mom was looking for me and couldn't find me. The authorities lied to my mom and wouldn't tell her where they were keeping me. I really don't know what they told her but by the time they found me I had lost a lot of weight and had become very ill with a fever of 105 degrees. The medication they gave me made me even sicker. My mom eventually got a lawyer and found me, and I was released. Finally, I could feel the warmth of the sun, and the taste of the air was sweet. I was free.

I enjoyed it for a few days. And then I went to the Us Organization's office on 78th and Broadway and joined.

4

"TAIFA TIME"

Us came together as an organization officially in September of 1965, a few weeks after the Watts Uprising. Before that, it had been like a study group, meeting at the Aquarian Spiritual Center on Santa Barbara Avenue, now MLK Blvd. Aquarian was a bookstore—the oldest Black bookstore in the country—and center for Black people to come together and find information on metaphysics, science, astronomy. It was a community center where different groups would hold meetings and individuals would hold lectures for the public.

Aquarian was started by a couple, Dr. Alfred and Bernice Ligon. The bookstore continued to operate until 1992. It had moved from its original location within the Spiritual Center, on the corner of Santa Barbara and Budlong, to an apartment building up the street closer to Normandie. At some point, for some reason, they moved from there into a shopping center at King and Western, where they were, unfortunately, sadly, burned out during the Rodney King Uprising. They rebuilt but the store closed permanently two years later. Bernice passed away in 2000 and Dr. Ligon passed away two years later.

The Us Organization stood for Black Cultural Nationalism. It stated that Black people within the United States were an African people who were distinct and separate from others. It would be through the return to our own unique Pan-African cultural heritage (along with some modifications) that we would be able to free ourselves from white oppression. The co-founder and leader of the organization was a man named Maulana Karenga. He was just twenty-four years old when the organization first started, had a degree in political science from UCLA and was a brilliant theorist. You might not think that to look at him, though. He was light-skinned and shorter than the average man. He had a slender build and kept his head completely bald. His mustache came down the sides of his mouth to his chin, but he didn't wear a goatee. It looked like a horseshoe pointing downward; what people called Fu Manchu–style. His voice had a sort of high squeal to it. You wouldn't think he had command of so many people who were willing to do his bidding, but he did. He said his first name in Kiswahili, an East African language, meant "master teacher" and his last name meant "keeper of tradition." It was under Karenga's leadership that a relationship began with the poet and activist Amiri Baraka and the Congress of African People (CAP) in Newark, New Jersey. Both CAP and Us played major roles in the Black Power Movement at the same time as the Black Panther Party for Self-Defense. The development and spread of the Pan-African holiday Kwanzaa was also developed during this time period, all under the leadership of Karenga and Us. And it was under Karenga's leadership that Idili and I would be held and tortured for three days at his home.

A few months before Us officially started, Karenga asked Kicheko Davis to start a dance group for the organization—the Taifa (Nation) Dance Troupe. Kicheko was part of a group of people, many of them students from Pasadena City College, who attended the lectures and programs of the group at the Aquarian Center and became the first official members of Us. Kicheko had been a dancer since she was a little girl, studying classical, modern, jazz, and ballet. She was basically a ballerina, just not professionally. Kicheko soon added African dance to her resume after learning from the South African singer Letta Mbulu. Mbulu was born and raised in Soweto, South Africa, and had been singing and touring since her teens. In 1965, while performing in New York with a troupe that included her brother Philemon and husband Caiphus Semenya, the trio refused to return to South Africa with the others. They became artists in exile to protest the country's racist apartheid system. They were able to meet up with other South African artists like Miriam Makeba, Hugh Masekela, and US jazz musician Cannonball Adderley. Next, the trio found their way out to Los Angeles, where they worked with Masekela, and Mbulu eventually recorded a few albums.

Various individuals housed them, some in Hollywood, some not, who supported their exile, and at some point, they met Karenga, who asked them to teach dance classes in the Black community. Kicheko trained with them daily for about six months. They taught her how to do the "Boot Dance," which was a dance the men would do. It started from the men who were forced to work in the diamond mines in South Africa. They would have to wear these rubber boots that went all the way up to their knees, like firemen's boots, because the mines had water in them. To pass the time and keep their morale up they would sing and dance. The boot dance was one of the art forms they created. They were basically enslaved in those mines, but they created an art form just like the blues here, when our people were enslaved or sharecropped or worked on the chain gang. Same thing. They also taught the Zulu dance, where the men kick their legs up high and stomp. They taught dances that the women did, other dances from Africa, and they taught songs as well.

I think that when people think of African dance the image is usually of women, regardless of ethnicity. In my opinion, the Taifa Dance Troupe was very popular in LA and elsewhere partly because we had male dancers. Not just any old males either; a lot of these brothers had been in gangs before they joined Us, much like in the Panthers. A lot of them were, you know, "street." There were tall brothers, muscular brothers, brothers who you ordinarily wouldn't cross if you saw them in the streets. And we had them with their shirts off, jumping around, coordinated and rhythmic, telling stories of the Motherland. They were doing "warrior dances," the kinds of dances they would do in Africa before enslavement and sharecropping and Jim Crow and conked hair had ever been thought of.

But that's just my opinion.

It was August of 1967, just before the Watts Summer Festival, when I ended up joining the dance troupe. I went to Us's office, which was housed at the Black Congress. The Black Congress was like a united front of a lot of the Black organizations in LA at that time, and it had this building on 78th and Broadway. Us, the Panthers, the Community Alert Patrol, SNCC (the Student Nonviolent Coordinating Committee), and a few other groups all had offices there. The Black Congress was the idea of a man named Walter Bremond. He was the guiding force behind it when it started in 1962. By 1968, he had spearheaded the creation of another organization, the Brotherhood Crusade. Walt believed that Black people had to do for themselves, which meant they had to fund their own organizations and programs. That way, there'd be no confusion as to whose interests a group or organization was working for. It was because of Walt and his work, along with others, that the National Black United Fund (NBUF) would be created. NBUF is the reason that payroll deductions can now be channeled to Black nonprofit groups. Before that, only white groups like the United Way would get those donations. Walt and Karenga had been friends since before Us was created. He died in 1982.

The year after the Watts Rebellion and Us started, in 1966, the Watts Summer Festival was created that August by a man named Tommy Jacquette. Tommy had been part of an organization called SLANT—Self-Determination and Leadership for All Nationalities Today—that also worked with Karenga before the founding of Us. After the rebellion, Tommy, who chose the name Halifu ("resist/rebellious"), became one of the co-founders of the Us Organization.

The festival was intended to bring about healing in the community and a new beginning after the rebellion. In the second year of its existence, the Taifa Dance Troupe made its official debut at the festival. Taifa also made an appearance on a 1968 episode of The Rosey Greer Show, which added to its visibility before things began to get really heavy. The show was well received and added to the praises we had been receiving since its inception.

Rosey Greer was a popular football player for the LA Rams in the mid-1960s. After he retired, he had a nighttime variety show on ABC. The show also interviewed local LA folks, spotlighting community affairs. The show first went on the air in June of 1968, around the same time as the assassination of Robert Kennedy, who was running for president that year. Greer and Kennedy were friends, and Greer was acting as a bodyguard that night for Kennedy's wife when RFK was assassinated. Greer is one of the people who tackled Kennedy's assassin, Sirhan Sirhan, wrestling him to the ground and taking his gun away from him.

But before that, I had gone to the Black Congress building, walked in, and Karenga just happened to be there that day. He turns around and looks at me like "WOW," like that kind of look. We talked for a while and he said, "I'm gonna give you a name that nobody else has." I told him, "I already have a name, Deborah. It means 'to be.'" He says, "No, you're Tetemeko." Tetemeko, hmm, I thought. "What does that mean?" He said, "One who makes the earth move." And I thought, Okay, I kinda like that.

It was obvious he was interested in me, but as far as being interested in him, I wasn't. I looked at him as a little short, bald-headed man. He had no appeal to me, no charisma as far as I was concerned, and once I found out he was already married, that sealed it. Besides, I had a secret crush on Amiri (General) Jomo, the head of Us's security arm the Simbas, even though he, too, was older and married. Jomo was light-skinned like Karenga, but tall and slender. He didn't wear his head bald either. He wore a short natural, a mustache, and a goatee. He was quiet and serious and respected by everyone in the organization.

When I met Karenga, he tried to convince me to be his fourth wife. That would never work for me. Karenga thought I was just a beauty, young and dumb. I really didn't like him hitting on me. I'm like, "This old so-and-so, such-and-such, hitting on me, UGH!" In truth, Karenga really wasn't that old at twenty-seven, but to me as an eighteen-year-old, he was ancient!

I don't know why Karenga focused on me, but I'm guessing it was because I was educated, came from a household with a mom and dad, but also had a little bit of "street" since I had been in juvenile hall. I don't know. I guess I had a good combination of qualities he had been looking for.

I realized later on that I had been to Karenga's home once before. Somebody took me to this house on Brynhurst. It was like a big African party going on but laid back. And I remember I danced. I loved dancing. I danced most of the night. I don't remember being tired. I just enjoyed the music and danced. I didn't know any African dances, though; I would just move my body to the music.

I had always liked to dance, but it was in Taifa that I learned African dance. I found out that in the beginning Kicheko, the first director of the troupe, also didn't know African dance either. She was learning via Letta and Cephus. But she was in charge, so she would have people audition with whatever they knew, and modern dance was close enough to African dance. Basically, Kicheko wanted to see if folks had a sense of rhythm, and that became the standard for all the auditions.

Once accepted into Taifa we would rehearse five days a week. We went everywhere to perform. We performed at the Hollywood Palladium once. We would go all over the state, visiting Berkeley, Stanford, and San Diego. We went out of state back east. Within that first year we went many places. I felt like I had found my niche. I felt comfortable, at ease. And, of course, I got to get away from Los Angeles and my mom. Being in the dance troupe rehearsing, performing, traveling, I wasn't around or involved in any of the Us Organization's day-to-day operations. At the time, I didn't know what the other women inside of the organization were going through. I didn't have a clue of the suffering. In the dance troupe, I didn't have any duties or responsibilities. My job was to dance. It was a pretty big group, about thirty of us, male and female. We might be in Washington, DC, dancing, we might be in Berkeley, we might be in Philadelphia. We danced for Black students, other Black organizations, and some white progressive organizations too.

I was gone for a whole year that first year when I joined, and it was wonderful! That's another reason I didn't know what was happening with the women in the organization. When I came back to LA and finally settled down to really observe, it blew my mind.

In the beginning, I was so happy to join the dance troupe I rushed out and started "dressing African." Amiri Jomo, the one I had a crush on, was married to a woman named Tamu. I remember her being very traditional African, very beautiful with her shaved head. She wore necklaces over her breasts and most of the time she was barefoot. For me back then, I considered her to be Mother Africa.

We were communal in the dance troupe, and we'd see one another pretty much every day of the week. It was the most fun part of Us for me. One of the people who played drums for the Taifa dancers when they first started was a man named Mtume ("messenger"), the musician who people know today from the song "Juicy Fruit," but he was gone by the time I joined. We also had a brother named Damu ("blood") who would narrate alongside our performance, telling a story about our dance. Every dance told an African story: how the ancestors lived, or a love story, or a story on how we were taken. The dances always told a story.

We were celebrated for our talent, and we would meet all kinds of people, but the majority were deans, administrators, and students at universities, especially ones with Black Student Unions (BSUs). But I always had a feeling as if we thought we were special and had a haughty, proud attitude. Although we traveled a lot, I don't remember a lot of sightseeing. Maybe because we usually rehearsed almost all the time. From rehearsals then to the stage. Whenever we traveled to a city, we never stayed there more than one day.

A sore point for me was that I don't remember ever being paid for performing in the dance troupe. That just would not do after a certain point. Sure, I enjoyed the experience; we were fed and didn't have to worry about housing and transportation, but eventually reality set in that I needed some money. So, I refused to dance anymore. This was in 1969, just before the troupe ceased performing altogether.

I remember there being a lot of jealousy in Us because everybody was trying to get Karenga's attention as the leader, male and female. And here comes this new kid—me—right in and Karenga's kind of attracted to me. And he's talking with me and he wants to be in my company. So, I faced a lot of jealousy.

Haiba, Karenga's first wife at the time, was there but I didn't get any jealousy from her. Haiba is the one who really laid a foundation in the organization, not just for the women but for the organization as a whole. Haiba had been in the Nation of Islam; she was in the MGT (Muslim Girls' Training) unit, so she was disciplined and organized. She knew how to put a thing together. There were Karenga's two other wives also: Mashiriki (Gail Davis), who was the youngest; she later went by the name Idili. She would end up being tortured with me, and Tiamoyo, who is Mexican. She was convicted right alongside Karenga for being one of our torturers.

Anyway, I ended up walking away from Us after that first meeting. About three months later, I started going back around the organization seriously, met Kicheko, and became associated with Karenga. I wasn't interested in him romantically, but he took a liking to me and began to open up to me. He starts telling me about his childhood. He told me about his brothers. He told me that he was the seventh son out of so many kids. He told me about how he and Haiba got together. He just started talking to me. I guess he felt at ease with me.

But there was still that issue of mistreatment that crept into the dance troupe. What I didn't like about the dance troupe was how the men made the women feel. We would be on the road, stopping for dinner, at a rest stop, and it seemed to me that the women were always serving the men first and they would get what was left over. The men were always over the women. But I didn't feel like they were over me.

I took note of all these things because that's not what I thought I was joining. I had my own place. I was calling myself grown. I had graduated from high school. I started working and wasn't living with my mom and sisters anymore.

I was involved in Us via the dance troupe, but I wasn't involved in the organization. But when I finally got home and really got into the organization and really looked at what was happening, I made it a point to tell Karenga he was wrong. It seemed to me like no one in his inner circle would go against him.

But I did.

5

WOMAN/WARRIOR

"WATTS STILL SEETHING"
"1965—When the riot cry was 'Burn, baby, burn!'
"1966—Why the ghetto today is close to flashpoint"
"THE YOUNG LIONS"
"In shirts labeled "Simha"—Swahili for lion—young militants are drilled in Watts."

The rest of the country—and possibly the world—was introduced to the Us Organization's Simba wa Changas ("Young Lions") when four Black boys appeared on the July 15, 1966, cover of Life magazine. The boys, who looked like they were preteens, stand erect with shoulders straight, facing forward with a fierce focus. Two of the boys in the back appear to be looking directly into the camera. A Black man with dark sunglasses and a goatee, wearing what looks like an olive-green dashiki-type garment, stands to the side behind them, obviously shouting commands. A web search of this image shows the magazine went to a subscriber in Sapulpa, Oklahoma. I wonder what thoughts went through their mind when that issue came in the mail?

Simba was the term for the young men aged twelve to about twenty-five in the organization. Men up to about age fifty or so were called Saidi ("lords"). After that, they became Mzee or Elder. Young girls in the organization were called Malaika ("angel"). The women in Us—late teens, married, or "marriage age" and older—were called Muminina, which meant "true believer." Like in most situations, the women really were the backbone of the organization. Mumininas or "true believers" were committed and used their skills and talents in service to the organization.

Whether a woman had a particular skill or not, she could still expect to be—and most likely would be—in a relationship with a brother. Each man in the organization was expected to have a "house." This was the woman he was married to. The women were the "house" because it was in the home where women provided a foundation and stability. But the man was always considered the head of the house. Married men could also be in relationships. The woman on the side was considered his "side woman," or just his "woman." She was not his "house." I learned all this later after I left the dance group and transitioned into being a day-to-day member.

A woman was not supposed to be in the Us Organization and remain single; she was supposed to "belong" to a man. I say "supposed to be" because I wasn't romantically involved with any of the men in Us while I was there. I belonged to no man. I was no one's "house."

Once I came back to Los Angeles and started going to meetings and gatherings, Karenga, who had already expressed an interest in me, began to confide in me. We would talk sometimes when I would go by the Black Congress office, or before Us meetings started, or afterwards while people milled around. I don't remember the context for the conversation but in the spring of 1968, I mentioned to Karenga that I knew about weapons and had received training. He told me to go and see Amiri Jomo about being in the Matamba Tribe.

Matamba was an area in present-day Angola, Southwest Africa. It was once ruled by a queen named Nzinga. But she didn't just sit around on her throne. She physically led the warrior class to defend themselves and drive enslavers out of the country.

Jomo thought the idea of having women as soldiers in Us was a good idea. He took the idea to Karenga, who agreed. Jomo then selected eight women who he would train to be the first members of Matamba sometime in 1966. Those women would subsequently train all other women members with Jomo's assistance. I don't know who those first members of the Matamba were. I know Kicheko was a member, but by the time I came back from being in the dance troupe she had left.

Matamba women undertook the same training as Simbas: sleeping out in the forests of California, hunting for food, horseback riding, weaponry, martial arts. We learned strategy, tactics, and security protocols. We learned how to search people for weapons at the weekly public forums that Us held called "soul sessions." We would search all the women attendees for guns. Whatever the Simbas did, we did. Sometimes we trained and did maneuvers together.

When a lot of people say that Us was a cultural nationalist organization, they say it with this attitude that cultural nationalism is nonthreatening and has nothing to do with revolution. But Us was clear that a cultural revolution would, by definition, overturn things that were taken as status quo, so we would need to be prepared for the inevitable violent reaction and retribution. Us and its advocates—the label given to people who joined the Us Organization—always maintained that a violent revolution would need to be preceded by the cultural one. People used to say, "We need to get our minds right so we'll know who to shoot when the time comes."

Sometimes, brothers within the organization also needed to get their minds right.

I once heard a story, I forget from who, about how some of the brothers in the organization thought that they could hit the sisters in the organization. You know, slap them around. Well, they could not. It was three of them, three different men in the organization, all around the same time period but not at the exact same time. The story goes that, one by one, these men were lured into an alley, or caught in an alley, and the Matambas beat their asses in that alley. After that third ass whipping, Amiri Jomo called on the sister who was over the Matambas at that time, whose name I don't remember, and told her, "We need a truce because I can't have you beating up my Simbas." The sister agreed and the brothers learned their lesson for the time being. They learned that retaliation was absolutely on the table, and the Matambas cooled out.

When I went to see Amiri Jomo like Karenga said, I went to his home and saw all his weapons, and I got excited! I've known about weapons since I was a little girl, about eight or nine years old. My dad taught me, of course. He even gave me my first gun, a .38 revolver, after I was tortured. My mom, a country girl from Louisiana, also taught me a couple of things about guns when I was growing up. Once, when my daughter was about five, I gave her a stopwatch, and when I was ready, I told her to press it. I broke down and reassembled a .357 Magnum in twenty-five seconds. I think that was too slow.

When I was at Edison, I met a boy at my father's store in Downey named Carl. His family invited us to visit them on some farmland they had in Northern California. Carl and his older brother and sister would teach me about hunting and killing animals, how to strip them and cure them. My sisters Valerie and Felecia weren't really interested in that part of the trips to the farm! I was fortunate in that I've always had some adults or older kids around me who taught me things and didn't try to take advantage of me. I had a very wide knowledge base even though I was still young.

That may be why Karenga didn't treat me like he did some of the other women in Us. He didn't treat me like Idili; she was his "secretary" in the organization, and he also considered her as a wife. There were a lot of things I didn't know about in the organization until I really started paying attention. Sometimes you're just naive. But I was also coming from an entirely different worldview. I was coming from two parents who taught me to broaden my world beyond 78th Street and San Pedro. Some people never left the neighborhood to go anywhere. We traveled to Florida, Tennessee, New York. We went to Yosemite, the Grand Canyon. I was up in Yellowstone with my family when people in South LA wouldn't even go over to Norwalk. My parents always told me, "The world is yours." How many people in the 1950s were taught that as girls? Little Black girls? Very rare. Even my friend Debra Tate, her dad owned a business, but she didn't go anywhere. My family was among the first, if not THE first, to walk into Disneyland. We were in places that would not even consider Black people. We were riding horses and skiing and fishing. I learned to swim at the age of four. There was no limit to my world just because I lived on 78th and San Pedro, thanks to my parents. My dad would take us to museums, and we visited several of the Spanish missions all the way up to San Francisco. I had a whole different take on life. I already thought I was a queen by the time I was fourteen (That may have been part of my problem!).

I was always taught to be a leader by my parents, never a follower. That wasn't the norm when girls were being taught to be nurses and secretaries and housewives. I was taught to be something different. So, with that attitude, Karenga decided I should be the Nzinga of the

Matamba Tribe.

There can only be one queen anywhere at any given time. There could only be one Nzinga. And once I became Nzinga, I wanted that power to help Black women in that organization. I don't know if that was Karenga's plan, but it was mine.

Once I became Nzinga, I insisted that all women in Us undertake Matamba training, whether they were interested in joining or not. I just felt like they needed that training regardless of what their actual duties were in the organization. I let the men know they had to respect the women in Us, their sisters in struggle.

One time, I saw where the men were fed and the crumbs belonged to the children and the women. You heard me. The women in the organization would have to stand behind the chairs and watch the men eat. I didn't know that was taking place until I saw it with my own eyes. Another night, I was at a gathering, and I watched a guy point to a woman that he didn't even know and say, "I want to have you tonight. You're gonna have sex with me tonight." Those kinds of things.

No more. No more telling women "You're going to sleep with me." No more cooking and feeding men first.

The thing about the training is that it gives women a sense of self-esteem. A feeling of confidence, an increased confidence to what they already had. A lot of the sisters in the organization weren't putting up with men's crap anyway. You would always hear something about "so-and-so left," or "blank-and-blank broke up." They didn't need my help! But the Matamba attitude just made the women fiercer. Not that they could just take on any man and whip his ass, although there have always been women who can do that. But a kind of, "I know what I will accept and what I won't accept, and I'm no longer accepting that kind of treatment."

I had no control over what people did in their homes or relationships, but when they stepped into the Hekalu, the organization's temple, or office or meeting spaces, whenever we had events or meetings or gatherings, that would be no more. There would be no more mistreatment of women like that in the organization; I stopped that nonsense.

At least I thought I did.

6

1968–69

I was away from Los Angeles for about a year. I left the dance troupe at the same time it ceased functioning. When I got back, I was able to see what was going on. 1969 was the year that things began to fall apart in the Us Organization. As in most things, though, the seeds of Us's unraveling had been planted before they actually blossomed.

Lots of people outside of Los Angeles don't really know anything about the Us Organization. None of the people who were actually in Us have written any books, and very few people who have written books on the Black Power Era have actually talked to Us members. But before it all fell apart, Us had a lot of respect among Black people in Los Angeles. People respected Us for the way members carried and conducted themselves and what they believed in. Black people in Los Angeles supported certain organizations because of their programs and what they espoused, and they supported Black organizations overall because they were working in some way for the betterment of Black people. Us had a lot of support, the Panthers had a lot of support, SNCC had a lot of support in Los Angeles, and other local organizations, like the Community Alert Patrol. We were all Black people in the struggle for Black people. That was the atmosphere during those days. Plus, it's not like Us members were strangers or anything like that. We were all from here. Grew up here, went to school here, hung out at the same places, even dated each other and had some fights with each other! We had done all of these things before we became Us members.

These same people that think they know about Us think they know about the Panthers because of the books people have written. But I actually knew some Panthers because I went to school with some of them. They lived or hung out in my neighborhood. One of my high school boyfriends was involved with the Panthers. Everybody knew everybody.

For the most part we all got along with one another, individually and organizationally. But during this time period, people and organizations were fighting for Black peoples' allegiance. People were fighting for Black peoples' hearts and minds. No organization can do anything without people who believe in what the organization is doing. So, rivalries developed.

Some of these rivalries were friendly, often boiling down to who had the best line or rap that Black people would gravitate towards. Who could pull more people from the street. Some of the people in Us, primarily brothers, had been in gangs or lived in neighborhoods that were rivals of gangs or neighborhoods that brothers in the Panthers were in. But there were also people inside of the Panthers, and inside of Us, who had been in rival gangs. Some people were of the opinion that they were the only ones that had the correct and true way to liberate Black people, and all others were punks. All of this was independent of the government's plan to wipe out Black organizations.

The government's counterintelligence program, COINTELPRO, just played on and exacerbated all these rivalries and turned them deadly. People also talk a lot about how the government destroyed such and such organization. They don't talk enough about how such and such organization helped the government to destroy them. Helped with their own destruction.

Us wasn't supposed to be a mass organization with hundreds of people joining it. Karenga's plan was to influence other organizations to adopt his ideas and ways. That's the nice way of putting it. In reality, it looked more like taking over other organizations and running them. That didn't always go over well with these other organizations. It left some hard feelings.

So, all of this was happening, while at the same time, Karenga was pushing Black organizations in LA for some kind of unity. Operational Unity, Karenga called it. On the one hand you're saying we can and should all work together without believing in the same thing; on the other hand, you start to act like you're the only game in town and no one else matters. What could go wrong?

When I first met Karenga, he and I would talk about different things. He confided in me, I guess, because he thought I was going to be one of his wives. I wasn't, but I would listen to him anyway. He told me he needed medication because of his eye. I don't remember what he said was wrong with his eye but that's why his glasses were tinted. He said his eye would cause him a lot of pain at times, so he would take placidyl for it. I remember he showed me a prescription pad he had. He bought it from some doctor for $1,500 and he could write himself a prescription for any drug he wanted. I don't remember all the drugs he'd use, but placidyl was one of them.

Lots of people, lots of them, were using hard drugs in those days. I can't say everybody was using them because that's just not true. I hadn't started to use them, for instance, until after I was violated. But when people say everybody, they mean it was so widespread that it was almost like it wasn't a taboo. So many people, people you would be shocked to know used drugs, people in the liberation movement. Lots of them.

Just like "regular" people who used drugs, people in the movement used drugs. And just like "regular" people, some people could handle drugs better than others. Karenga used drugs like other people used drugs. Sometimes for pain, sometimes to get high. But too much drug use caused a problem. When things started getting heavy with the Panthers; when the rivalries became fights and violence; when the police, which would hassle Us just like they hassled the Panthers; when the police began telling Karenga that Panthers were out for him and telling the Panthers that Karenga was out for them; when people started getting shot and killed, it wasn't just silly paranoia. But the drugs made it even worse. Karenga was receiving death threats from different places: Panthers, people in the community. I found out later, even people in Us. The majority of threats came from the government. We know that now, but not for sure back then. You didn't know who or what to believe.

A lot of things went down while I was away from LA. I remember that night, just before I joined Us, when a bunch of us were all hanging around the Panther office and the police came and grabbed us all up. I had never experienced anything like that before. I learned later that was a regular occurrence at the Panther office. They'd be harassed by the police all the time, day or night. But when I joined the dance troupe, we were out of LA so much, I never knew that was going on. I don't remember hearing about it or people talking about it while we were on the road.

I learned later the government's threats and harassment were crude and corny. Some people who were around then could figure out which threats were real or were from cops and the government, but there were a few who actually believed the lies. Bunchy was the main person who would meet with Karenga and Jomo about cooling things out.

Bunchy was a diplomat. He really was like the Mayor of the Ghetto. He was the leader of the Slauson Renegades and the leader of the Panthers. Anything the Panthers couldn't handle, the Slausons could. But he also worked for Black unity, which is why he would always meet with Karenga to try to cool out any friction caused by the government. Another reason for the government wanting him out of the way. And then there were the police attacks on the Panthers.

The crude and corny threats came from the government, but the local police weren't that corny. They were how the government carried out its plan to wipe out Black organizations like the Panthers. There were lots of raids, shootings, and shootouts in 1968. And then Bunchy and John were killed at UCLA. During this time Karenga had strong ties with the poet Amiri Baraka in Newark, New Jersey. He was in New York or New Jersey when Bunchy and John were killed, preparing to speak at an event Baraka had organized while chaos was raining down in LA. The police immediately raided and locked up dozens of Panthers they said were planning to "retaliate" against Us, which was a lie. The news about Bunchy and John reached Karenga as he was about to speak to the crowd. Baraka said that Karenga looked shocked. We were all shocked. Many of us were hurt. Bunchy was a good brother. I never met John, but I only heard good things about him. The whole thing was a horrible tragedy.

The government wasn't satisfied with Bunchy's and John's deaths. In May, the FBI set its sights on the Panthers' Free Breakfast program for children by raiding offices and shutting it down every chance they got. By the fall, the FBI had kicked up its hatred of the Panthers and directed all kinds of things to be employed against them. The main propaganda they disseminated was that Us was out to get Panthers, and that Panthers were out to get Us.

The Panthers had different spokespeople and leaders; they didn't really have one leader, like Us did. That meant that when threats were made saying, "So-and-so is out to get Us," what the threat really meant was that they were out to get Karenga. It was under this weight of drugs and drug-fueled paranoia that Karenga said that Idili, his fourth wife, and I, had tried to kill him. That we were trying to poison him. It was all crazy and it was all a lie. We weren't trying to poison him.

His response to that was to teach us—and everyone else—a lesson.

7

MEETING

Mother's Day weekend, 1970, was a typical, beautiful, clear and cool LA weekend. The temperature was around seventy degrees with blue skies and no rain. But that didn't mean that things weren't hot and heavy.

We were all still traumatized by the murders of Bunchy and John in January of '69 and Fred Hampton's murder that December. There was a lot going on nationally too. In early March, H. Rap Brown was about to go on trial in Maryland on charges of inciting a riot back in 1967. The night before his trial began, two SNCC brothers, Ralph Featherstone and Che Payne, died in a car bomb explosion on their way to attend the trial. Just blown up; the police said they were planning to blow up the courthouse, but people in the movement said they were assassinated. By the time May 1970 had rolled around, there would be the murders of four white Vietnam anti-war students at Kent State University in Ohio and two Jackson State University students over racism and police brutality in Mississippi.

Also in May, a new magazine had just come out for Black women. It was called Essence, and the cover was a close-up picture of a beautiful Black woman with a large Afro. One of the stories advertised on the cover of the magazine was "Revolt: From Rosa to Kathleen." The Kathleen was Kathleen Cleaver, communications secretary of the Black Panther Party and wife of Panther Minister of Information Eldridge

Cleaver

And then, there was my own personal horror story.

We didn't have anything major planned for that Sunday. Of course, my sisters and I would treat our mom to dinner, perhaps a movie and shopping; you know, the usual. My father had just returned from prison, and even though he would have been more than willing to help pamper my mother, I'm sure she would've been content to simply have stayed at home with him since he had been gone for so long. Whatever we were going to do that Sunday became moot. For me, time stopped that Friday night.

Friday nights in the Us Organization, we would gather at the "Sun House," Karenga's home in Inglewood, after work and meetings at the Black Congress. The Sun House was the home where Karenga and his first wife, Haiba, and their children lived. It was also where Idili lived since she was also a wife of Karenga. It was called the Sun House because "the Sun set and rose on Maulana. He was the center."

There would be informal get-togethers where we would just kick back, maybe talk about issues of the day, party. I had no idea that on this night I would be the star attraction. I did think it was a little odd that when I got to the house there were only a few Simba present. Other than Tiamoyo and Idili, there were no other women in the house. There was no sign of Haiba or the children, no members of the Matamba or any other advocates, although they had been present just a few hours earlier at the Black Congress.

Karenga had been real paranoid since the murders of Bunchy and John. Support for the organization in LA had fallen off, and nationally, people were beginning to look at Karenga differently. The Detroit-based Provisional Government of the Republic of New Afrika, where Karenga had been named a Minister of Culture for the Black Nation inside of the United States, kicked him out, and his relationship with the poet/playwright and activist Amiri Baraka in New Jersey had already begun to cool before Bunchy and John died. What a lot of people outside of LA didn't know, however, was that people within the organization had been quietly leaving since before that, as far back as '66. A lot of members felt that Karenga's ego was in the way. A few had even threatened his life. They believed in the vision and mission of Us so strongly that they felt that Karenga, their co-founder and leader, was the one standing in the way of realizing that vision! What's that saying? "Just because you're paranoid doesn't mean people *aren't* out to get you." It was like that.

With all this happening, Karenga told everybody that I represented the enemy. There may have been talk about others being enemies also; all I know, all I remember, is that he was now concentrating on me. He had already told people in the organization not to talk to me. He told them a whole bunch of stuff, so I became isolated. The fact that I had never been shy about voicing my opinion did not help my situation.

I didn't hold my tongue about how I felt about things, and I was not interested in Karenga romantically. Those two things had been the recipe for the disaster that was to come.

When I was in Us, I maintained my own outside associates. I had a life outside of them. I had my own apartment, my own money. I had my own back, my own independence, and that was one more thing that Karenga was angry about. It really bothered him. It came down to the fact that I was a leader inside of an organization I had no business being in; I wasn't a follower. And Karenga got it in his head that, among other things, I wanted to take over his organization.

The next to last straw for Karenga, not the one that finally broke the camel's back, was when I went against him regarding Haiba. It appears that no one else had ever done that, publicly disagreed with Karenga, or had done it and been allowed to stay in the organization.

I wasn't just outspoken for the sake of it. I'm just a caring individual. I cared about the women that were mistreated. I cared about the children who weren't getting fed correctly. I cared about women who were being turned out sexually. And I let my feelings be known. The other reason I did that was because that's what I thought we were supposed to do, as Brothers and Sisters. *That's why I'm joining this thing in the first place, right?* I'm thinking this is why I'm joining, to be able to express these things. And if I see wrongs, to make sure that we correct them so that it can be a better organization. And Karenga hated me for that. He hated me when I stood up for his wife Haiba. I don't know exactly everything that happened between Karenga and Haiba, but he hated her. And he hated me for sticking up for her.

I remember very clearly one evening, there was this big meeting at the Sun House. Karenga was talking about having Haiba, his first wife and the mother of his children, killed. He was going on and on about how women should stay in their place, and how they must show more deference to the Black man as the head of the family in the home and as the leader outside of the home. I mean he was really gone, and so many of the people present agreed with him on what he was talking about. Everyone was like, "Yeah!" And I was like, "NO!" I mean, you're going to kill the mother of your children because she doesn't bow down to you??? I said, "No, no, no . . . Mm-mm . . . That's not working for me." And Karenga looked at me. The room was silent, waiting to see what would happen next. I remember him glaring at me through those black-rimmed glasses. No one said anything. Karenga didn't say anything; he just glared for only a few seconds, but it seemed like an eternity. He changed the subject from Haiba specifically to something about male-female relationships in Africa, trying to justify what he had just been saying. He never forgot or forgave me for that. From that point on, I was a marked woman.

I don't know what all went on between Karenga and Haiba, but it was something that wasn't cool. Before the night he had talked about killing Haiba I had heard rumors: one was that she had been kept in a tiger cage in the garage. *A cage.* A metal cage covered in chicken wire in the garage. I had seen the cage before, but I never saw Haiba or anyone in it. I heard from more than one person that Haiba had been put in it. I found it hard to believe, but enough people told me about it. I don't know how many times she was supposed to have been in there, or for how long, but I think it was more than once. The cage wasn't huge; it was big enough for an adult to crawl into and sit or curl up in, but not stand up. I remember it was in the back of the garage and it had what looked like a dirty blanket inside. I hadn't heard about Haiba being in this cage when I first saw it. I just thought it was maybe for a pet of some type that Karenga once had.

Karenga's paranoia about me had been growing for quite some time. He had me followed to work and other places by certain members. He started having people threaten me, you know, "You can't leave." It was almost like a Jim Jones type of thing. It *was* a Jim Jones thing, basically.

As I mentioned before, it hadn't always been that way between Karenga and me. At first, he would talk to me personally about things like his childhood or his brothers. But I wasn't interested in him romantically, and I went against him. Many of the people in the organization were very loyal. I was seen as being disloyal, so that made everything change.

All of those things led up to the "grand finale." He said we, Idili and I, had tried to poison him. He claimed we took hypodermic needles and stuck it through the tops of soda cans and tried to poison him. Then he said that we put poison on the wall, and when he touched the wall he was poisoned. After that, he said we had put poison crystals in his food. It was hard to keep up with everything we were accused of. Whatever it was, this Friday evening of Mother's Day weekend in 1970 was the last straw.

I knew something was going to happen that day. I can't explain how or why I knew; I just knew. That evening, after most folks had left the Black Congress building, some of the Simbas from the organization came and got me. I don't know who they were, which ones came and got me. They claimed there was a meeting and that I should be there. But it wasn't a request. They had guns and made me go with them.

I had been feeling the temperature change for a while: a few of the members acting funny towards me, acting cold. Ordinarily I wouldn't care what people thought about me, but the energy in the tight circle of people in the organization that Karenga kept around him during this time was of serious paranoia because of Karenga's serious paranoia. Whereas many other advocates had either left or were leaving the organization because of Karenga and his personality, there were just enough that remained in the organization to stay loyal to him.

When they came to take me to the meeting something just said, *This is it.* I didn't try to fight them. There were too many of them and they had guns. So I went with them.

When I got to the Sun House Idili was already there. She was Karenga's third wife, so she lived at the Sun House along with Haiba and Tiamoyo. They brought Idili in and sat her down next to me on this black leather couch. *Something bad is about to happen,* I thought to myself. I leaned over to Idili and said, "This is it." She looked at me like, "What? What are you talking about?" I said, "This is it. Something's gonna happen." And that's when a couple of Simbas came in with guns and took us both out of the house and into the garage.

The garage was the torture chamber. This is where Haiba and the cage were kept when she was said to have been made to sit in the cage. That's when I remembered: I had also heard about two other people, both men, who had been "taken out to the garage." I never heard their names, what happened, or why, just that they had been there.

I didn't join the Us organization to find out that people needed to escape. I didn't know I would be someone who would need to do that. I had already begun to seriously wonder what kind of organization I was in. What had happened to the organization I was so happy to be involved in two years earlier?

I had started thinking about how I needed to just walk away from Us.

But I didn't move fast enough.

8

TORTURE

"INFIDELS!!!!!!"

Tiamoyo had this crazed look in her eyes as she screamed at us.

"How dare you!! INFIDELS!!!!!!"

"What are you talking about?!" Idili asked. She was as confused as I was.

"WHERE ARE THEY?!" Sefu, Fred Glover, growled at us.

"Where's what?" I said.

"The poison!" Tiamoyo screamed. *"The poison!"*

"What poison?! We don't know what you're talking about!" we both said in unison. They didn't believe us. There was nothing we could've said that would have saved us once we were in that garage. Even if we had known what they were talking about, we would've still had all manner of hell unleashed against us.

"Maulana knows you were sent to kill him," Tiamoyo yelled at us. "For the last time tell us where they are!!!"

"We told you we don't know what you're talking about!!!" I yelled back at her. That's when I knew: I could tell by her eyes something within her had snapped. Next thing I knew, *PAPP!!!* I was blindsided by a backhanded slap in the face by Seydu, Louis Smith. As quickly as I had been slapped, he grabbed me and Tiamoyo began tearing my clothing off. Fred was holding onto Idili from the back as Tiamoyo ripped every single thread I had been wearing off me. I stood there naked as Louis held me, struggling to break from his grip. Tiamoyo then moved over to Idili and began ripping her clothes off. They tied our wrists with rope and then hung us both up from the ceiling, our feet barely touching the ground. Tiamoyo started slapping and cursing both of us. That's when I had had enough and spit in her face. It was a nice juicy glob too, right at the corner of her mouth. That's when the men started hitting us. Not slapping, but punching us, with closed fists.

Louis and Fred were nineteen at the time, barely out of high school, but both had worked their way up the ranks of the Simbas where Maulana entrusted them with being Mwalimus (teachers) to the newer members of the Simbas. Fred had a very quiet demeanor. He wasn't bald like Maulana and several of the other men in Us. Louis' Afro was small, and his nose was broader. They were both of average height, though Louis was skinnier. They both wore these black combat boots with a very thick sole all weekend long. I remembered because I didn't usually see Fred wearing those kinds of shoes. He taught martial arts to the Simbas, so whenever I saw him, he was either wearing soft, flat shoes, like "kung fu" shoes, or he was barefoot. But for those three days Idili and I were being held, both Fred and Louis had on those boots. And neither of them ever took them off.

POWW!!!

I took a fist to my right jaw. I don't know which one of them hit me. I had never in my life been hit so hard. Unfortunately, I didn't pass out. If I had been fortunate to pass out, I would've been spared everything that came after.

FWAP! FWAP! FWAP!

Louis had a long outdoor extension cord doubled in his hand, whipping both of us on our naked backs. He was whipping us fast, crisscrossing: forehand, backhand, forehand again. Imagine a child getting a whipping. Or a runaway from the plantation who had been caught. The pain was unbearable.

FWAP!

We were both screaming and wriggling around. I couldn't stay still as Louis whipped me. No one could. But I also wasn't going to just do nothing.

WHOOSH!

I swung my body around and tried to kick him in the face as hard as I could using both legs. My thighs and legs had always been strong from where I used to run track. I thought, *If I can just get one good kick in, either knock him out or knock him down and away from me, maybe I could work my hands free.* I kicked out, and I missed as he quickly stepped to the side. That's when Fred grabbed both my legs to keep me from trying it again. He tied my ankles with rope, then Louis took a karate stick—one of those nunchucks—as Fred held my legs out for him. Louis raised it high above his head then brought it down on my left foot.

WHAM!

Then, he did it a second time.

WHAM!

I screamed from the top of my lungs. I thought, If I'm going to die I'm going to make them work for it. Louis leaned in close to me, glaring like he was going to taunt me. I guess he was going to ask me again about those damn nonexistent pills or crystals. As soon as he got close enough, I head-butted him as hard as I could. I sure did.

BAM!

"AAHH!" he yelled.

Amiri Jomo taught us, the women in Matamba, to use the head-butt as an absolute last resort. Lots of men who use the head-butt, they become almost immune to it because they practice it so much. Amir Jomo didn't suggest that we practice it repeatedly because, well, we were women. Even though we were trained to be soldiers just like the Simbas, there were still some holdovers from male chauvinism. No matter; we women weren't too keen on practicing it that frequently either. But I had to do something to try and disorient one of them, to see if I could get free.

I knocked Louis back a couple of steps. He held his nose as blood spurted through his hand. I hadn't knocked him unconscious or disoriented him. I had only made him madder.

POOM-POOM!

Two quick punches in my face, to my nose. I screamed as the blood spurted and started trickling down my mouth. He broke my nose. I wanted so badly to hold it, to try and squeeze my cheeks, try to calm the pain in my nostrils, but I couldn't. My hands were hoisted high above me, and I just could not break free.

There was a workbench with a vise attached to it next to where Idili and I were hanging. Fred grabbed my legs and Louis took my right foot and put my big toe into the vise and started turning it. I screamed and squirmed and cursed them, trying to wiggle my body free. But that only made things worse.

Idili was being worked on by one of the men as I was being worked on by the other. Tiamoyo was overseeing them, going back and forth to the house through a narrow door in the garage. I could hear Karenga's voice as she reported to him. He hadn't joined in yet; they were just getting started.

Much of what they did to me, they also did to Idili. They rigged up some battery-thing to shock us with. It was a piercing, stab-like feeling. At one point they took me down from the ceiling and held me on the floor. They stomped on my back; to this day I still have problems with my back.

And then, they took turns raping me. Sticking things in me.

I don't remember. I just wanted it to be over.

Ssssss

It sounded just like the hot comb my mom would use to press my and my sisters' hair when we were little. I used to think the smell of burning hair was awful. That was before I smelled burning flesh.

Ssssss

Idili's scream was gut wrenching. I don't remember how long they held the soldering iron against her cheek or which one of them did it. I just remember that sound: *Ssssss*.

They held it there long enough for it to turn a long, slender section of Idili's brown-skinned cheek black. Then crinkly. Then pink. I heard that same sound when they put it in her mouth, and it touched her tongue and bottom lip.

Ssssss

Idili wasn't raped, however. After all, she was Karenga's wife, so that wasn't going to be permitted. But that soldering iron, the beatings, and a water hose stuck in her mouth, trying to drown her; Idili suffered just like I suffered.

We suffered together from that Friday night until Sunday, Mother's Day afternoon.

Despite all of that Idili still wanted to stay. She wanted to stay with Karenga. A lot of Jim Jones' people wanted to stay with him too. You know what I'm saying?

Karenga would drop in and out during the torture session, checking to see how his stooges were progressing. At one point, when I was laying on the floor, Karenga came and sat on my stomach and thighs as someone held my hands over my head, pinned to the ground. I was in pain, in agony, trying to hold on until it was over, whatever "over" meant and however long it took. Karenga leaned in close to my face and sneered. "Trying to kill me? Gonna poison me, huh? Where are they? Where's the rest of it?" he demanded to know.

I turned my face away from him and ignored him, trying to will the pain in my body away. "ANSWER ME!" he thundered, grabbing my chin and yanking my face back to look in his eyes. I could feel his fingers digging into my aching jaws; they had been softened up by Louis' and Fred's punches. He was hurting me. But I didn't cry. I wouldn't cry. My mother's voice was too loud in my head: *"NEVER LET THEM SEE YOU CRY."*

That's when Karenga told one of them to bring the water hose. One of them brought it over as Tiamoyo rubbed some laundry detergent into my mouth. Before I could spit it all out, she grabbed the water house and stuck it into my mouth. I coughed and spit. I wasn't aiming at anyone in particular; I was just trying to get it out of my mouth. Tiamoyo moved from me over to Idili and did her the same way.

Tiamoyo was there the majority of the time in his place. She would do whatever Karenga said to do. They're actually twins. The ones torturing me, Louis and Fred, had stopped talking.

Idili and I were a bloody mess. On the last day, when everything was over, Karenga came back in. He told them to cut the ropes from our wrists and Tiamoyo to give us our clothes. Karenga himself led us to the door and said, "Take Deborah to Angeles Forest and kill her." And then, almost as soon as he said it, he said, "No, let them go." Just like that, in that order. We walked out. Idili was like, "I don't want to go." "Nevertheless, you're out," I told her.

And we started walking. One foot in front of the other.

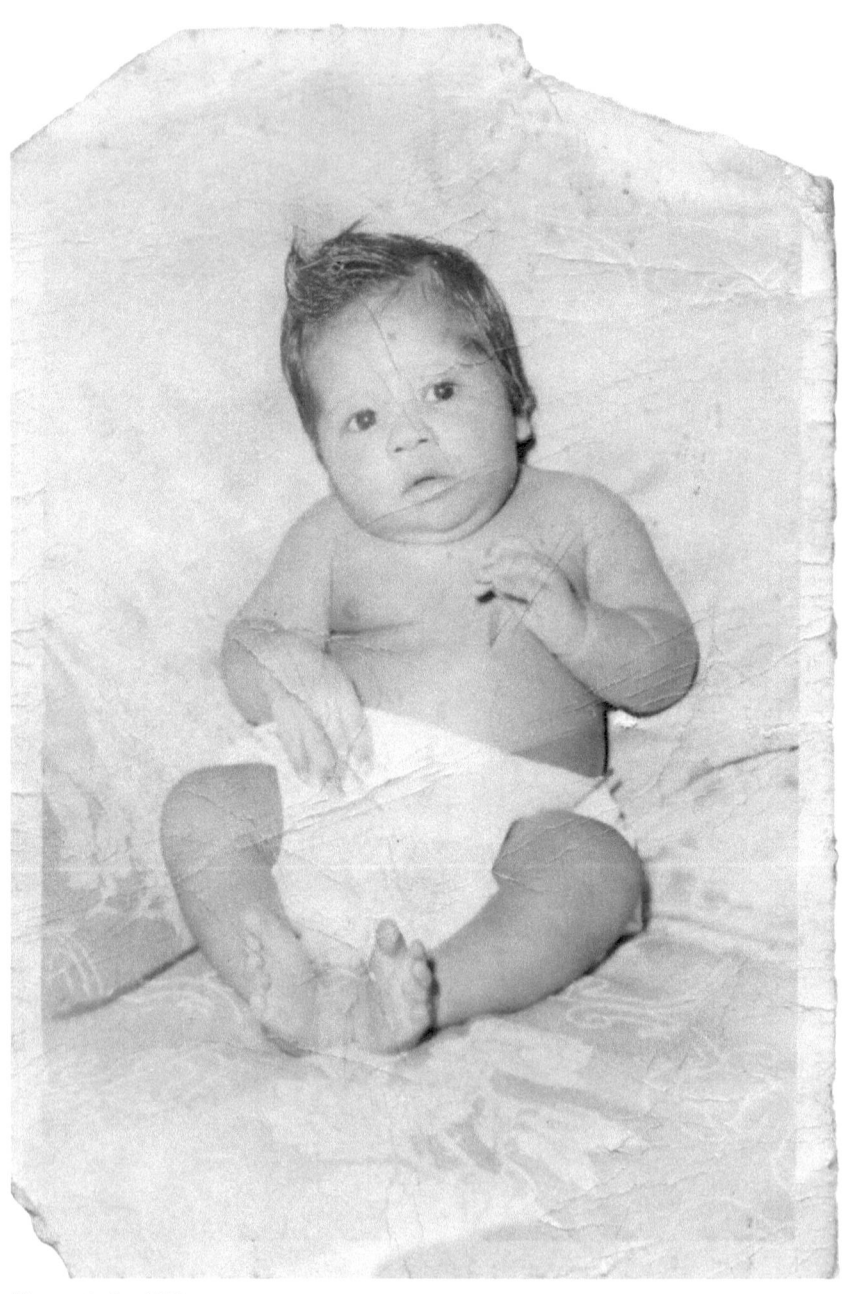

Me as a baby, 1950.
Courtesy of Deborah Faye Jones.

Me and my sisters Valerie and Felicia.
Courtesy of Deborah Faye Jones.

Me on horseback, 1954 in Beverly Hills.
Courtesy of Deborah Faye Jones.

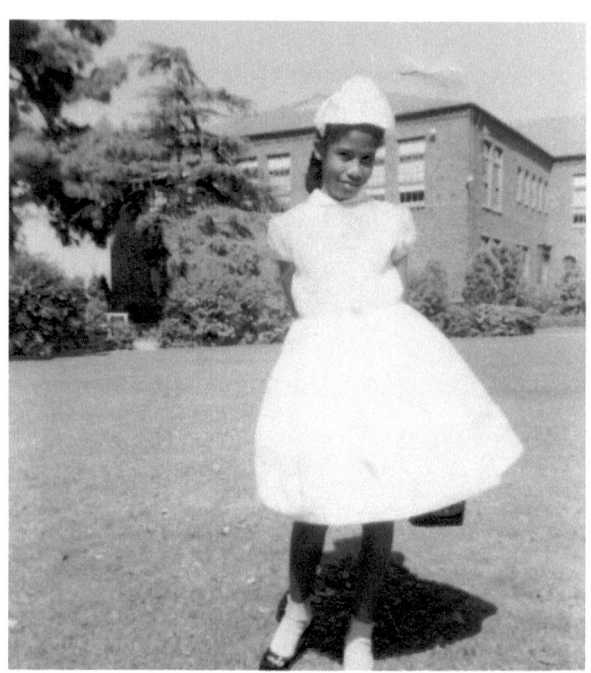

Me in my Sunday finest.
Courtesy of Deborah Faye Jones.

At Yosemite with my mom and my two sisters, 1961.
Courtesy of Deborah Faye Jones.

Mildred Faye Stone, my mom.
Courtesy of Deborah Faye Jones.

Mildred Faye Stone, my mom.
Courtesy of Deborah Faye Jones.

Frank Jones, my dad, received an undergraduate degree while in prison.
Courtesy of Deborah Faye Jones.

Me age 12.
Courtesy of Deborah Faye Jones.

Shani Maisha Scott, my beautiful daughter, at age 16.
Courtesy of Deborah Faye Jones.

Obituary of my beautiful daughter Shani Maisha. We reconciled and were very close for several years before she passed away.
Courtesy of Deborah Faye Jones.

Henry Pierson Scott. "Perry," age 28, when we first met. My lifeline.
Courtesy of Deborah Faye Jones.

Terry Williams, my husband, who I met after Perry.
Courtesy of Deborah Faye Jones.

My precious Shani Maisha, at age 5.
Courtesy of Deborah Faye Jones.

In my 40s while being a teacher. My smile hid the turmoil underneath.
Courtesy of Deborah Faye Jones.

My sisters Felecia, left, and Valerie, on the right. I was 13 at the time.
Courtesy of Deborah Faye Jones.

In my 40s while being a teacher. My smile hid the turmoil underneath.
Courtesy of Deborah Faye Jones.

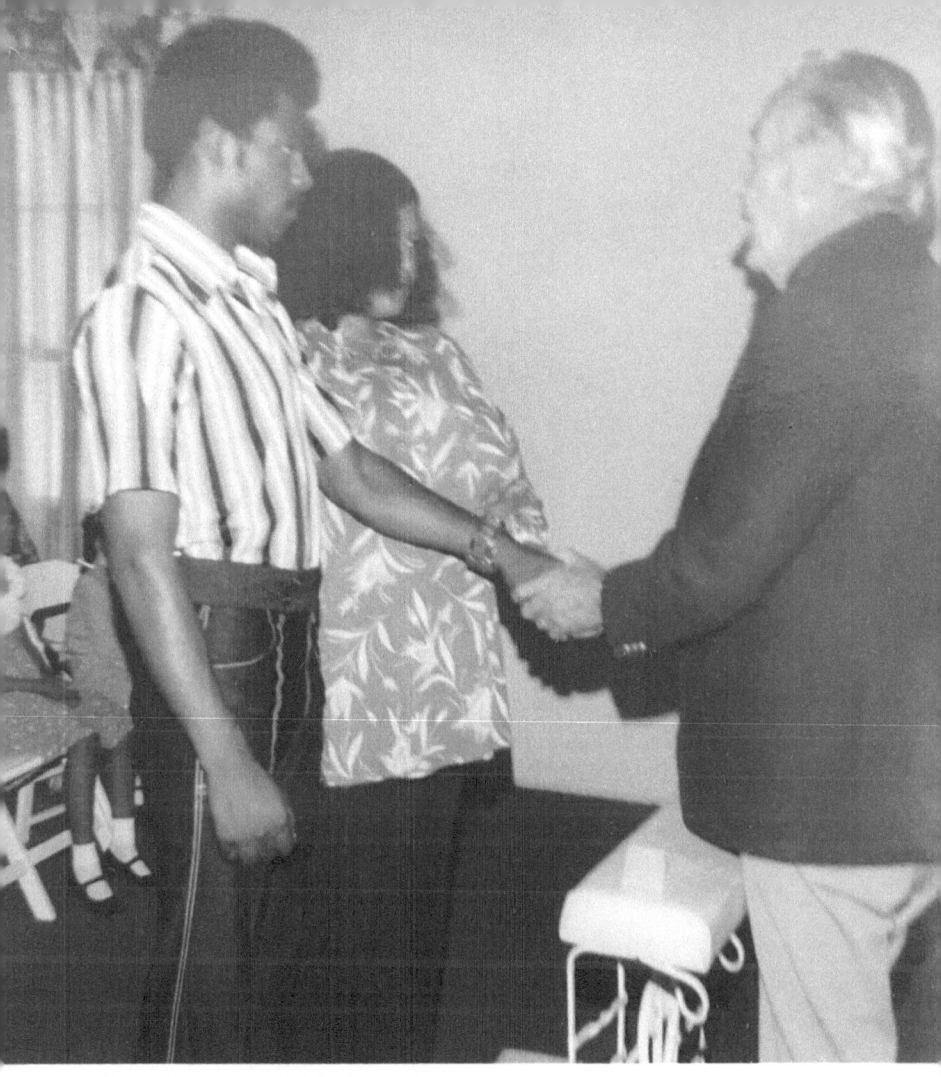

Terry and I renewing our vows in Inglewood.
Courtesy of Deborah Faye Jones.

At Cal State University Northridge for my oral history interview. Finally at peace.
Courtesy of the Tom and Ethel Bradley Center, CSUN.

9

RELEASE

Everything felt so heavy as we trudged along. Our footsteps were pregnant with the past, present, and future. They were reminders of the hell endured, a task to be completed swiftly, and a promise of freedom.

One foot in front of the other.

We plodded west towards Los Angeles International Airport and access to the beach. Beaten... bloody... hurting... but alive.

One foot in front of the other.

"Sista Tetemeko! Y'all need a ride?!" Joseph yelled as he pulled his car over across the street from us. Joseph was one of the newer members in the organization. He had been driving down Century when he spotted us. Robert, another new member to the organization and Joseph's roommate, was in the car with him. Nichole, Robert's girlfriend, sat in the back seat. I didn't know Nichole well. I had seen her at a few events with Robert, but she hadn't become an advocate yet. At that moment I didn't think to tell her not to join, to run for her life and not look back. I was too preoccupied with my own survival.

Joseph and the others were heading east, coming back from the beach when they saw us. Joseph's eyes were normal when he asked if we needed a ride from across the street. It wasn't until he had turned the car around, pulled up next to us and hopped out to open the door that I could see the shock on his face, trying to process what on earth could've possibly happened to us.

"We were in a car accident!" I blurted out as soon as I saw his eyes widen. "Can we stop by your place to get cleaned up?" Joseph and Robert shared an apartment in Inglewood on Budlong Avenue, not far from where we were. We would still be in some proximity to Karenga's house but that was a chance Idili and I had to take. We needed to find a doctor and then get as far away as possible.

Idili and I got into the back seat with Nichole. As a rule, whenever Us men and women traveled together in cars, the men sat in the front and the women sat in the back. All male Us members under the age of twenty-five were automatically members of the Simba wa Changa, "Young Lions." They provided warrior training to the men in the organization. As Simbas, sitting in the front seats placed them at a better vantage point to be able to deal with any situation that jumped off, or so we were told. We were told that by being in the back seat we would be less of a target. But we would also be able to provide backup to the brothers should they happen to need it because it would be unexpected. In the beginning, the women of Us were simply groomed to be servants to the men. Of course, they didn't say it like that; they never do. They dress it up with flowery language. "What makes a woman appealing is femininity and she can't be feminine without being submissive," was one of the quotes from Maulana that was drilled into us. It was the man's role to be the warrior and do the fighting, and it was the woman's role to serve the man and mind the children while looking sexy by wearing big Afros and long flowing dresses.

Once we got in the back seat, I wanted to scrunch down low as we passed Crenshaw Blvd., but I couldn't. The pain in my back was horrible. That's where Fred and Louis had taken turns whipping, kicking, and stomping me.

We were going to pass by my job at a specialty store called Zody's at the intersection of Crenshaw and Century. It was similar to a small Walmart and lots of Black folks shopped there. I used to think it was cool because it was just a few blocks from the Sun House, and I could walk to work whenever I stayed there overnight.

I had a check waiting for me at my job—the job that hadn't seen me in over forty-eight hours—but I didn't want to try to get out of the car just yet. I asked Nichole if she would go in and tell the manager I was sick and pick up the check for me. Check in hand, we headed toward Joseph and Robert's apartment. Since I couldn't scrunch down low, I had to sit upright. I hoped and prayed that I wouldn't see any of our assailants. I hoped that none of them would see and recognize us or Joseph, and that neither Joseph nor Robert would want to stop by Karenga's house first before getting to their apartment.

That was a lot to hope and pray for. I closed my eyes and imagined myself disappearing into the cushion. I wished myself invisible and kept my eyes closed until we got to Western Avenue, about a mile away. That's when I got the idea to ask my godmother Eva to cash my check for me so I would have some cash. I asked Joseph to pull up to a pay phone on the corner so I could call her since I needed money to put my plans in motion. The car pulled into the parking lot but when I tried to exit I couldn't. My damaged feet and the unbearable pain in my back made me yelp when I tried to get out of the back seat. I decided to save all my strength for just getting out of the car once I got to their apartment. "Do you all want to go to the hospital?" Nichole asked. The look on her face was almost as incredulous as Joseph's. "Yeah, but I need to call my godmother first," I told her. Nichole said she'd make the call for me and got out from the back seat.

Joseph shared a first-floor apartment on the east side of Budlong with Robert. Fortunately, there was a parking spot directly in front of his door and I wouldn't have to travel too far. I needed both of their help getting out of the back seat. It took every ounce of strength I could muster not to scream. The pain was searing down my leg and radiating back up into my lower back.

Even though we had accepted a ride from them and we were going to their apartment to get cleaned up, which required a lot of trust, I didn't really want to trust them. They were too new to be fully indoctrinated into the cult from which Idili and I had just escaped. Neither of them had ever personally done anything to me, but I couldn't trust them because of who they were as advocates of Us. Us was a cult of personality and the personality was that of Maulana Karenga. Under his direction, Idili and I had been held and tortured for the last three days by two of his advocates, including his wife. We had been labeled and punished as traitors who had conspired to kill Karenga. Since Idili had been one of Karenga's wives, I guess he spared her, but he had actually told some of those advocates to kill me.

My mind raced along with thoughts of conspiracy. Zealots are pretty much the same everywhere. What if someone had seen us riding in the car with Joseph and Robert on Century? What if someone decided to call Joseph once we got to the apartment? What if someone decided that Idili and I hadn't been punished enough?

I wouldn't feel safer until we got out of that area. We quickly washed as much blood off ourselves as we could, but we were still battered and bruised, and our clothes had rips in them. Nichole loaned us some African print fabrics to cover ourselves in. My left hand throbbed and wouldn't do anything I asked it to do. I found out later that three of my fingers were broken. The underlayer of skin on Idili's cheek was a bright pink. Nichole wanted to gently wipe it with a cloth, but Idili jumped when she moved toward her. No more pain, at least not until we got to a hospital. Nichole gently put a glob of Vaseline over it as a layer of protection instead.

"Where's your car, Sister?" Joseph asked me. I was deep in thought, analyzing possible scenarios and countermoves when he asked me. I just looked at him blankly. He repeated the question; that's when I remembered, *Oh yeah! That's right! You told him we were in a car accident! Get your lies straight girl! They know these aren't normal car accident bruises; they know something's up!* Fortunately, if they thought otherwise about the source of our bruises, they never said anything about it.

"Right over on Inglewood Avenue," I replied.

"You want us to go take a look at it? Go get it?" Robert asked. "No, no, it's cool," I answered. I didn't want to take the chance that he or Joseph would stop by Maulana's house first to see if anybody there could help retrieve my mythical car. "My priority right now is getting this money and getting to the hospital. I can get the car anytime," I told them. I don't know if they believed my answer, but they didn't ask about the car anymore. We all piled back into Joseph's car and headed towards downtown LA to where Eva worked. Joseph, Robert, and Nichole were quiet the entire drive. Whatever it was they were thinking, they kept it to themselves.

Eva was a hatmaker in the fashion district of downtown LA. We pulled into the company parking lot on the side of the building and there she was, a light-skinned, heavyset middle-aged woman with brown hair, waiting on us. Nichole had told her about the car accident over the phone but as soon as I stepped from the car, and she saw our injuries she actually fainted. Robert was able to catch her before she hit the pavement. Now three of us needed assistance. I knew Eva, once she recovered, would be on the phone to my mother. I wasn't sure who else she'd call and I didn't want to deal with all that. I wasn't ready to deal with all that. I had to think, to plan.

To be truly safe, I needed to get out of LA.

We got Eva situated, assured her it was just a crazy hit-and-run accident and nothing more. I was able to get my check cashed and got out of there before she could call my mom. I'd have to deal with my mom's reaction, but at least I wouldn't have to deal with it just yet.

LA's county hospital is a few hops, skips, and jumps from downtown and city hall, right at the border of East LA. Hispanics/Latinos were the majority population in East LA, while Blacks had been concentrated along Central Avenue going south from city hall. My mind was racing. I didn't want to stay around Joseph, Robert, and Nichole much longer; I didn't know what might happen, but I also wasn't sure what could happen. Since it wasn't too far, I made the decision that we should walk to the hospital.

We thanked Joseph, Robert, and Nichole for dropping us off at Eva's and we started on our way. If those three thought our injuries weren't from a car accident, the doctors at the county hospital knew it. "A fence fell on us," I told one young white male doctor with black hair and thick, black-rimmed glasses. Don't ask me why I went with that lie and I didn't stick to the car accident—I was under a lot of stress. He didn't verbalize it, but his eyes said he didn't believe me. Those doctors got us together. I had a cast, Idili's facial wound was dressed, and they gave us both some prescriptions for the pain. They also called the cops. About an hour or so after we got to the hospital both the police and a couple of Us members showed up, almost at the exact same time. I was sitting on an exam table nearest the hallway when I saw them casually walk down the hall. Us members, especially the men, had distinctive looks. Those bald heads or short Afros, stern looks, and of course

African dashikis. Most of them wore talismans made in the shape of the organization's logo. I laid back on the table and pulled a sheet up over me. Idili was behind a curtain, across the aisle from me. I prayed she would stay still and not make a sound. We didn't stay to find out who they were or who told them we were there. We didn't talk to the cops either; we went quietly out the hospital's back stairs and slipped into the afternoon's setting sun.

We made our way to a motel further into East Los Angeles. The two twin-sized beds with weathered and thin blankets may as well have been queen-sized with royal goose down pillows and comforters. We didn't care. We needed sleep and time; and this was where we would get both. I called Idili's grandparents in Oakland and told them about the car accident and asked if Gail—that's what they called her—could stay with them for a while. "Of course!" they replied. We weren't that far from a Greyhound bus station, so I told Idili we'd get on one the next day to the Bay Area. She agreed and soon disappeared under the covers. I was familiar with the "soft" snores I heard coming through her blanket. It was the kind of sleep that came from exhaustion, where you fell asleep not because you're sleepy, but tired and just plain worn out. I needed the same kind of sleep, but it was eluding me.

The lights from the taco stand across the street from the motel stayed on all night long. I know because I watched them flicker until dawn began to appear. I tried to sleep but I couldn't still my mind. I needed to rest, but then I needed to plan. I needed to plan, but then I would remember that I needed to get some sleep. I'd close my eyes but then be awakened by noises like an aluminum can inspecting its surroundings, or locals moving about the motel parking lot in search of meals or hidden treasures. Or other motel patrons settling into their new homes, and temporary lovers on the clock. I'd hear a noise and sit upright. Was it a Simba coming for Part Two, unfinished business, sent by Karenga or his evil twin, Tiamoyo, Karenga's wife? She was a Mexican woman with a huge Black Afro. She was supposed to be our sister. We were told she was our sister. I would wonder, How could she help them do this to us?! But she was Karenga's wife, and she did what he told her to do. Then my eyelids would start to close again, and I'd repeat everything all over again.

I knew there was no way to keep this from my parents. I just wanted time to figure out how I was going to handle it. I wanted to keep them out of it, keep them safe, but I knew they would do just about everything they could, not stay out of it. My dad had only been home a few months from San Quentin Prison, where he had just done eight years. He would want to handle it his way, a way that more than likely would send him right back to San Quentin. My mom would have ideas of how to handle it too, but I knew it would be nothing as extreme as my dad. But I wanted to handle things on my own. I wanted to be the one to exact revenge on Karenga, but I would need time and a plan.

I didn't go straight home to my parents since Us members had followed us to the hospital. I was afraid they'd try to do something to them and/or my sisters, so I went up North with Idili. I got her situated with her grandparents and I stayed with a friend for about a week. But something just told me to come back home. I don't know what it was. I just wanted to be home with my family. I came back and stayed with them for about two months.

My mom was the one that called the police and pressed for charges against Karenga. She said, "He's going to go through the court system."

We called the police and they came to the house to investigate. They took pictures of my body, with all my wounds, for evidence. Then the media came. It was like a little circus. I was concerned for my parents, but I made the decision to do what my mom told me. I made the decision to testify against Maulana Karenga. When it came time for trial that's exactly what I did. And Karenga's first wife Haiba also testified against him. She came all the way from Virginia, where she had gone to escape his abuse, to LA to testify about what she had seen and heard about that weekend. She didn't have to do that. She could've said I want no part in this, but she didn't say that. Idili, however, decided not to testify. She was just too afraid. Us members had threatened to kill her family, so she wasn't taking any chances. "You just say it; you tell them," she told me. I understood Idili's fear. I was afraid for my family too, of course. I wished that they were removed from it all, that they didn't even know what happened.

My mom wasn't afraid, nor was my dad. I knew he wouldn't be afraid. I'm surprised he acted as tame as he did. But that didn't last long. I came home from work one day and sat down in front of the evening news to find that an explosion and fire had rocked the building that housed the Black Congress on 79th and Broadway. Although it had been a meeting place for a number of Black Power organizations in the city, it had fallen under Karenga's control in the last couple of years. "You know that was your father, right?" my mom said to me all casually as I watched the report. I hadn't known it, but I wasn't surprised either. I was grateful, not that he had "avenged" me, but that this, to my knowledge, was the only act in which he had allegedly engaged.

I tried to resume my life once I came back from Oakland. I didn't seek nor was I offered any type of counseling for my ordeal. As in most cities, rape crisis centers didn't appear in Los Angeles until the middle 1970s, a few years later. Looking back, I don't even know if I would've accepted counseling if it had been offered. But it wasn't, and I didn't take the necessary time for myself to heal. I went right back to work because I had my own apartment that I liked, and rent had to be paid. I didn't want to move back home permanently; I liked being out from under my parents. Besides, there was still the issue of my family's safety. I didn't want anyone trying to get at me and taking it out on my family instead.

I didn't trust anyone from the Us organization after that. I don't recall if any of them reached out to me, but I wouldn't have accepted anything from them if they had. If I had been on fire, lying in the gutter with my skin peeling off of me, I wouldn't have wanted one of them to spit on me to save me.

I went back to work even though I was a mess. I couldn't think. My whole life felt turned upside down. And I didn't know what to do about it. I avoided interviews and media presence at all costs. I refused to talk to them under any circumstances because I was concerned for my family. Members of Us had followed my sisters when they went to school. These were high school girls. They don't know anything about anything, and they had nothing to do with my relationship to Karenga and Us. They didn't deserve to be targeted. Thankfully nothing ever happened to them, but at that time I had to assume the worst. I knew what Karenga could be capable of. Idili and I weren't the first ones to be hung up and tortured in his garage and I'm sure we weren't the last before he went to prison.

I knew what the organization was capable of, but I wasn't worried for myself. I worried for my family. I had begun to isolate myself. Slowly I began to pull back from my job and from my family. I stopped going by the house. I just stayed away.

10

TRIAL

I got Idili situated with her grandparents in the San Francisco Bay Area. I stayed with a friend in Oakland for a couple of weeks, then came back to LA. I still hadn't figured everything out yet, hadn't processed everything, but I wanted to come home and be with my family. So that's what I did.

It had been two weeks, but my bruises were still fresh enough to horrify my family. Bones healing, but still broken. My sisters and my mother were hysterical. I don't remember ever seeing my mother cry before. My father had murder in his eyes. Both of my sisters were crying. My middle sister Valerie was very upset over what happened. At the time I didn't realize how much of a profound effect it had on her; it may have even exacerbated her mental illness. To this day, she gets emotional about it. Several decades later, while we were speaking on the phone about something, she brought it up, the torture, again. She was upset that our parents hadn't gotten me counseling with a psychiatrist.

After all those years it still bothered her.

After my parents saw all the bruises, they called the police. My mom's response, once she had calmed down, was, "We're going to put him through the system. We're going to have him arrested and put in jail," she said.

"That's not what I want," I said. "I want him to die. I want to kill him. I feel like strapping some bombs on and going over there like a suicide mission," I told my parents. That took them by surprise. They had never heard me express such sentiments about anyone before. But I had never been violated by anyone like that before.

Both of my parents' mouths were wide open, although I suspect for different reasons. My mama was probably shocked and horrified that the daughter she had hoped would be a debutante one day could utter such a thought. My dad was a little shocked, but I suspect he felt a momentary bit of pride in his eldest child. But my idea wasn't practical in my mother's eyes. Destroying myself in the process of getting back at Karenga would render the whole process moot. The objective would be to exact justice. So, the safest option—the one that was not supposed to destroy me, my mother reasoned—would be to call the cops on him.

The police came to our house and took down my story word for word. They brought a photographer to take pictures of the bruises on my body, and I gave them the name of the doctors at the county hospital who first attended to Idili and me. It was reported in the media that I had failed to identify Karenga initially. That is not true. I told them from the beginning it was Karenga who was behind it; they asked me who had physically assaulted me, not who orchestrated it. He wasn't physically there for the majority of our ordeal, but he was always a few feet away, overseeing or giving orders.

Idili was still in the Bay Area when my parents made their decision. The police eventually tracked her down to get her statement, but she refused to speak with them. Idili told me to tell what happened to the both of us. I didn't find out until much later that her family had been threatened by Us members. She was too scared to testify or to return to LA.

I became the exact opposite. I began to look forward to testifying against Karenga. I wanted to tell what happened. I went from wanting to blow him to pieces to settling for going through the legal system. It was the thought of him having his zombies threaten Idili and her family and how frightened it made her, as well as knowing that some of his minions had been keeping an eye on my younger sisters, that emboldened me. "Come threaten my family like that, motherfucker... see what you get." I was so angry.

All the time and energy I had spent in that organization, all the work I had done, the commitment I had made. I believed in the value and the righteousness of what I thought we stood for, what we were supposed to be building. And for this to happen? To be violated so brutally on the word of an egomaniac, and to now have my family physically threatened? "Why you little bald-headed motherfucker... I want to see you try something. Come on with it!"

I was so angry.

It would be that anger, that trauma, that almost destroyed me.

Inglewood police officers as well as investigators from the district attorney's office arrested Karenga, Fred Glover, Louis Smith, and Karenga's second wife Tiamoyo Luz Maria on October 6, 1970. They were at the courthouse in Inglewood to deal with some traffic charges when the cops got them. A grand jury indicted all of them on four counts of felonious assault, two counts of assault with a caustic chemical, and one count of conspiracy to commit these and other offenses.

Taking them to trial sounded easy. I guess it would to a person who was not familiar with the inner workings of the court system. No one told me about all the delays that go on.

Among the first delays was a warrant for the arrest of Karenga and Tiamoyo. They both failed to show up for their arraignment the day after they were arrested on the charges and the judge revoked their bond and issued the warrants. Then the judge reinstated their bond the day after bringing them in because Karenga told him he had mixed up the date when they were supposed to appear. He and Tiamoyo remained free while Fred and Louis remained in jail. The trial was set for October 20, 1970.

The next delay had to do with Karenga finding a lawyer to represent him. Karenga said he couldn't afford an attorney, so one was supposed to be appointed for him. That should've been easy, but the public defender attorneys kept citing "conflict of interest" because they were either currently representing Panthers or had done so in the past. Finally, in December, Karenga found a lawyer to represent him.

It had been seven months since Idili and I had escaped from him.

January of 1971 brought a slight surprise. Karenga and each of the other three had been charged with two counts of assault with a caustic chemical. A different judge from the one in the beginning dismissed those charges against all of them because he said there was "insufficient evidence."

I guess I should've grabbed the box of detergent they used on me as I was leaving the garage.

Another trial date set. More delays. Finally: the trial began in May 1971. It had been one year since Idili and I had escaped with our lives.

In his opening statement the district attorney basically said that Karenga was running Us like his own personal security force because he was paranoid that everyone was out to get him. And by everyone he meant people on the outside as well as inside the organization, such as Idili and me.

Haiba, Karenga's now former wife, backed him up on that. She had left Karenga sometime after Idili and I had been tortured and moved to the East Coast, but she came back to testify against him. Karenga said he didn't know why she was testifying against him and saying those things against him. Sure, of course he didn't. What a liar.

Haiba said she heard screams coming from the garage. She said that in order to get into the garage Karenga and some of the Simbas had to pass through the bedroom. She said she had gotten up once and looked into the garage, and at that moment she saw Karenga punch me in the face. She also said that she had seen him sit on Idili's stomach, put a water hose in her mouth, and turn it on. Karenga's attorney, this guy named Richard Walton, said Haiba was angry at Karenga and jealous of Tiamoyo, which Haiba denied.

Haiba didn't have to come to back to LA. She could've stayed wherever she was, kept quiet, and lived her life. Either she knew the horrific truth and felt she needed to do right by two of her African sisters, or she hated Karenga with the passion of a thousand burning suns because of something he had done to her; perhaps it was having been kept in a tiger cage in Karenga's garage. Either way, it didn't make him look good to the jury that his ex-wife, who had given birth to three of his children, was testifying against him.

According to the newspapers, I testified "unemotionally" when I was on the stand. I told the court how we were stripped naked and beaten with a cord and a baton. They were shown the photos of the wounds on my back that the police took. I told the court how they put my big toe in a vise. How Karenga threatened to shoot us. How they repeated their treatment of Idili and me over the entire weekend. All the while I was testifying, Karenga was looking at me through those thick, black-rimmed glasses of his. And I met his stare right back. I had to relive everything over for a group of strangers, what I had already been reliving privately and trying to forget. Excuse me if I wasn't "emotional" enough.

His lawyer tried to say that I was lying because, at first, I didn't tell the police it was Karenga who did this to us. That's not true. I had always said Karenga was behind it. Idili was so scared for her family that she refused to testify, but I wasn't. Karenga had people follow me and my younger sisters around to intimidate me. I was concerned, because I knew what they were capable of, but my parents assured me that they would be fine and that I had to testify against Karenga. "He's the one who needs to be scared," my dad told me. That eased any fears I had. My dad did not play around when it came to his family.

His lawyer also said that I testified against Karenga after the district attorney dropped charges against me for grand theft. That was absolutely a lie.

My parents and I left after my testimony. I wasn't going to hear his lies and sit quietly. That would've disturbed the court and caused problems, so it was best that we got out of there.

The newspapers reported that Karenga denied everything. No, he didn't beat us; no, he didn't order us to be beaten; and no, he didn't accuse us of trying to poison him. He said that Idili and I left his house voluntarily, looking for "other lodging," and that we looked "healthy" when we left. We looked healthy? You mean I wasn't bloody and limping, and Idili's cheek wasn't peeling off when we left? I couldn't believe it.

At another point in the trial, Karenga said Idili and I were suspended, that's why we left the organization together that weekend. But no reason was ever stated in court for why we were suspended. Because we weren't. We weren't suspended. We were tortured, beaten, and I was raped.

Karenga also said that if he had known that violence was occurring in the organization, like what Idili and I went through, he would've put a stop to it because the organization was against violence. He even said that Haiba had left and gone to the East Coast because he sent her there to rest, because she was "emotionally upset." What was she was emotionally upset about, Maulana? Nobody knows because Karenga's lawyer didn't ask, and Karenga didn't volunteer the information.

I've always been amazed at how some people are able to lie so effortlessly through their teeth and sleep so well at night. Amazed.

At the end, Karenga, his wife Tiamoyo, and Louis Smith were found guilty of assault and false imprisonment against me a little over one year after that weekend in that Inglewood garage. It was a Saturday, May 29, 1971. The jury had deliberated for five days. Fred Glover was found guilty solely of false imprisonment. All of them were acquitted of conspiracy, and all of them were acquitted of anything having to do with Idili. The trial lasted nineteen days.

Before he pronounced the sentence, Judge Richard Alarcon ordered that both Karenga and Tiamoyo undergo psychiatric testing. Alarcon is reported to have said that he wanted the tests to determine if what Karenga did was an "isolated act," or if he was truly a threat to society. Alarcon sat in that courtroom and heard that testimony and saw that evidence. His thought was that the jury should've convicted them of the same charges against Idili too, not just me.

Alarcon ordered Karenga to undergo testing in June, and he was sent to a state correctional facility in Chino. The next month, the deputy superintendent of that facility reported back to Judge Alarcon. The man, a guy named Achuff, wrote that Karenga "was a danger to society who is in need of prolonged custodial treatment in prison." Achuff's report said Karenga was irrational and behaved bizarrely, and sometimes he was "confused and not in contact with reality."

People always say how brilliant they think Karenga was. Well, brilliance has its pitfalls. Add in heightened paranoia—not completely unfounded—as well as the abuse of prescription drugs, and the criticism of most things white or European, and it's easy to see how Karenga could be labeled that way by the white folks' system.

But I didn't need their system to know that Karenga was a danger. To this very day, my foot, hips, and back remind me of how dangerous he was. I haven't seen Idili in decades, but I'm sure her face also bears witness as to how dangerous he was.

Friday, September 17, 1971. Sixteen months after that weekend in an Inglewood garage, Judge Alarcon sentenced Maulana Karenga to one to ten years in prison for torturing me. At that time, California had indeterminate sentencing in its prisons, which meant a range of time instead of a definite release date. Karenga had to serve a minimum of one year in prison. After that, the parole board would decide when he could get out. It could be after one year, two years, or after he had done all ten years. He ended up being released after four.

The trial was over. Karenga received punishment for what happened to me. My ordeal had finally come to an end.

And now, my descent into hell officially began.

11

DESCENT

Rape counseling was scarce, if it even existed, back in 1970. One of the first rape crisis centers ever created didn't come along until 1972, two full years after my assault. Private therapy never crossed my mind. While it may have been available, I probably wasn't even in the right place mentally to accept it, or to even withstand the stigma associated with it, which was so strong back then. I was so jacked up and damaged after my ordeal that I needed help, but I didn't know what kind, how, or who to ask for it. So, I self-medicated. Alcohol became my primary therapist, backed up by marijuana.

By the time the trial started I was drinking every day. I had gone back to work, but I was drinking and smoking weed more. Then, around the time that Karenga went to prison in the fall of 1971, I was raped again. After the attack at Karenga's, I stayed with my parents for about two months, and then I got my own place: a duplex next door to them. Later that fall, I came in from work one day in October 1971 and I hesitated before I went inside. I had been feeling weird all day, like something was going to happen, but I didn't know why, what, or where. Once again, I didn't listen to my intuition. I just shrugged it off.

I opened my front door and stepped into the vestibule. I hadn't gone more than a couple of feet inside the apartment when *BAMM!!!* I was hit the hardest I had ever been in my life, harder than when one of Karenga's goons hit me, on the side of my head and I blacked out. When

I woke up the side of my head was throbbing. I was bleeding from my ear, my clothes were torn, I had bruises on my breasts and wetness on my thighs and in my vaginal area. My apartment door was cracked but not widely. I didn't call the police or anyone else. I lay there on the floor for a while, dazed but aware enough to push the door all the way closed. I eventually got up, showered then crawled into bed. I never told anyone what happened to me, but I always thought it was the manager of the apartment building who raped me. He would see me and ask me out, to come by his apartment, to have a drink with him. Not every single day, but frequently enough to where it was annoying. Right after I was raped, he stopped asking me. Never asked me again. I have no proof it was him, but in my gut, that's what I have always felt, especially since he stopped asking me out. I certainly didn't tell my parents. Since I didn't have concrete proof, I wasn't about to lose my father to prison for committing a murder, because that's what he would've done. I kept it to myself.

A while after the rape I had to go to the emergency room. I was having excruciating pain, I was bleeding heavily outside of my usual menstrual cycle, and I had been having fainting spells. I would blackout and come to on the kitchen or living room floor. I was in such pain I thought I would die. I almost did die, in fact. My father would stop by to visit with me occasionally, and on this day I didn't answer when he knocked. We were supposed to go somewhere, and he and Perry, the man I had started dating, let themselves into my apartment and found me passed out. They got me to the emergency room, where I found out I had an ectopic pregnancy as a result of the rape. Instead of developing inside of my uterus, the fetus had been growing on the outside. That's what was causing the horrible pain and heavy bleeding. I was passing out from losing so much blood. I could've died.

I kept sliding down, deeper, into a hole, but for a moment, I was given a lifeline.

PERRY

I met Perry, Henry Pierson Scott, around the summer of 1970, and it was he who became my lifeline. My best friend Debra Tate introduced us. She was dating Perry's roommate, Tony Gleaton, at the time. She wanted me to continue my life and to get back on track. She didn't know the damage done to my soul. She was trying to pick me up and help me get back into a "groove." So, she took me to a party at Tony's apartment over near Fairfax and San Vicente. Tony was handsome and Debra was crazy about him. He was a student at UCLA, and later he became a very famous photographer of African Olmecs and how our African presence is everywhere. His pictures are in museums, including the Smithsonian. He became famous, but at this time in his life, he was a player!

When Debra and I walked into the party, it was going down! Beautiful people; incense; soulful, funky music; and dancing. Debra was taking me through the apartment by the arm when she pointed Perry out to me. Short and slender, Perry was fair skinned with reddish hair. He wore a medium-sized natural, and he had dimples. He was also going to UCLA, majoring in fine arts.

I first saw him at the party surrounded by women, but when he saw me and we made eye contact, he left those other women and came over and introduced himself to me. Honest, he did. I looked away from him for a second and saw that Debra had disappeared, just like that! It was just Perry and me standing there, alone in a room filled with dancing and swaying bodies. He was very flattering, but I wasn't really in the mood. I was damaged beyond my own understanding, damage that would last for years. But Perry was very kind and persistent, and his kindness and gentleness eventually won me over. We began seeing each other and I started falling for him.

Because of all I had been through I wasn't very interested in sex, but Perry was good to me and he was patient with me. So, I grew to respect him and to care for him. When I was finally ready to make love with him that first time, he was shocked when I disrobed. Scars from where I had been whipped and beaten covered me, from the backs of my ankles, up my legs, thighs, buttocks, all the way up my back. He asked me what happened, and I said I would tell him one day, but not now. He wanted to grab his coat right then and there and go find the person responsible for inflicting such damage on me. I told him he didn't have to worry about that, and that I would tell him everything in time.

I was a total wreck. I had no counseling or psychiatric diagnosis after the torture, which is why I was drinking so heavily. And Perry tried so hard to satisfy me. He sacrificed his own life plans so he could work to support me and care for me. I tried very hard to love him, but when you are as damaged as I was and hating yourself, it's pretty much impossible to love someone else no matter how hard you try. But we stayed together because Perry would not give up.

SHANI

In 1972 I became pregnant but miscarried. I was told they were twins, and the loss gave me another reason to keep on drinking. Later, I became pregnant again, and this time when I told Perry, he put his foot down. He was adamant about me not drinking during this pregnancy, so I acquiesced.

On June 10, 1973, our baby girl Shani ("wonderful") Maisha ("life") was born! There were some complications: I had her by cesarean section, she was premature, and both of us almost died, but she was here! She remained in the hospital for two months with tubes and monitors attached to her, fighting for her life, but she was here! Her dad adored her, and when we finally brought her home, we didn't want anyone to breathe on her! Shani was life for both of us.

I felt an African name for my child was important. I wanted her name to have meaning. In my heart I was still militant, and I still loved Africa. Nothing, no person, could ever change that. Choosing an African name for my baby felt natural to me. When I gave birth to Shani, I felt it was a miracle after all I had been through. Shani Maisha, to me, meant the "wonderful surprise of my life."

As Shani grew, she seemed unusual to us. She walked early and she would take off her diaper and get on the toilet herself. Her first words? Instead of "mama" and "dada" she jumped on a table and pretended she had a microphone and said, "Jungle boogie get down get down." We were astonished beyond belief! Where did this child come from?!

Shani was the light of both of our lives. I loved and adored my daughter, and I tried to be a good mother, but I was fighting a strong enemy. My moods, my depression from my untreated trauma, took a toll on my relationship with Perry. With no treatment, things only got worse, and there was only so much verbal and emotional abuse Perry could take. So, in 1975, I left. I left Perry because of me, not him, and I took Shani with me so he wouldn't have to choose between working and babysitting. Of course, Perry protested at first. He was saddened, but he was also tired. He knew I would never harm our daughter, so there wasn't a big, drawn-out fight about my leaving with Shani. She was about two and a half years old at the time.

I found a nice apartment on 42nd Street near Manual Arts High School called The Castle. Perry worked and paid our rent and food and any babysitting fees that were needed, as well as anything else to make his daughter and me comfortable.

The Castle was a huge brick-and-stone apartment building. The managers of the building were a married couple and they had two daughters. I forget the parents' names, but one daughter was named Vivian, and the other daughter, Helen, remembered me from Fremont, and she and I became friends. Helen liked to go out to clubs and was always trying to get me to go with her. My only interest at the time was my child, my Princess. One night I gave in, had Perry babysit, and I went out with Helen. Wow! What a sight, a true meat market. Helen knew quite a few people since she was a regular. She introduced me to two guys who said they would cook breakfast in the morning for both of us! *Breakfast in the morning?* I didn't think so. I really hadn't had much of an adult dating life except for Perry. Meeting guys at the club was not my thing, so I caught a cab home and didn't go out after that for a very long time.

When I say I was damaged from what I had gone through, there was depression and alcoholism, yes, but there was also this rage. The Bible talks about wrath. In the immediate aftermath of the torture, I wanted to strap hand grenades onto myself and blow Karenga to pieces. The alcohol and the marijuana would blunt my pain, but it would also cool out my anger from time to time.

Karenga had been locked away for the past few years and the Us organization had faded from the scene. My anger hadn't disappeared though; it had just retreated deep within me. There was nowhere to focus my wrath—except Perry occasionally—so it just laid low, simmering.

And then, sometime in 1975, Karenga was released from prison. My mom showed me the newspaper clipping one afternoon when I had gone by to visit. He had done four years of his one-to-ten-year sentence. The anger that had retreated within me began to bubble. That bubble actually burst a few times over the years, but unfortunately, the one who truly deserved my anger was never anywhere around me at the time.

Sometimes I wish I'd had a crystal ball back in 1970. Knowing all the things that would happen after my torture would have been great (It also would've been great to predict the torture, but you know what I mean.). It would've helped me prepare and perhaps even avoid some things, but of course, I didn't have that. Everyone goes through twists and turns, ups and downs in their lives. Looking back now, I can see how so much of what I went through in the following years can be traced back directly to that Mother's Day weekend in the Sun House in Inglewood. I might not be able to prove it, but I can see it.

The following years passed by in a kind of haze. I went to work, cared for my daughter, and came home, occasionally enjoyed life as best as I could, and continued to self-medicate. I didn't visit with a lot of people outside of my parents and sisters. I hadn't been dating anyone, and I really hadn't had any interest in sex. All that changed in the late spring of 1977.

TERRY

I was working in sales at Bullocks-Wilshire, a clothing and home goods department store that had good-quality merchandise, but it wasn't so expensive that it would break you. I was coming back from a lunch break one day, taking my time and noting the sights and surroundings as I walked around near Wilshire Blvd. and Vermont Ave., when I came across a building under construction. I looked up and saw a bunch of guys working and one caught my eye. He was tall and slender but built muscular. He was dark-skinned and had a regular-sized natural tucked neatly underneath his hard hat.

He was walking along the scaffolding as I walked along Wilshire, and he looked down and saw me. When our eyes met, he smiled hello and I said to him, "You're going to be my husband." "What?!" he asked, either confused or because he couldn't hear me over the construction. Or both. "I said you're going to be my husband," I repeated, and that made him climb down from the scaffolding and come talk to me.

To be honest, I was a bit shocked that I had spoken those words to him. I wasn't that shy around men, but to call a man I had just met my "husband," when I had never wanted to be married in the Western tradition of marriage? I don't know what came over me, but when I saw Terry that day, I was attracted to him. I guess it was just time. He and I talked once he climbed down from that scaffold, and I gave him my phone number. He called me that night and not long thereafter, we started dating.

Of course . . . *of course* . . . I soon learned that I was not the only woman in Terry's life. He was involved with a woman who had several kids. I think I may have wanted more to win him than to really love him. I pressed him and said which one, me or her? Was there really a choice? To me there wasn't. He made his choice and our relationship grew. Eventually he moved in with Shani and me.

Terry was a gentle and kind man. He was nonjudgmental and I loved that about him. He adored me and treated me like the Queen I thought I was. He was my perfect King.

He and Shani also got along great. Terry was a wonderful "stepfather" to Shani. Shani loved her actual father, Perry, but she also loved Terry, this new adult man in her life. Shani called him "Dad-dy" probably because Terry was in the house with us and she saw him every day; when she would be with Perry, she would call him "Dad-da," a slight difference.

I continued to self-medicate while I was with Terry, but not as much. Also, when I was with Shani's father Perry, the trauma from my assaults was still fresh, so he took the brunt of my pain when I would lash out. By the time I met Terry there had been the distance of time and living with just Shani. Our relationship was not drama free, however. Sometimes you're a participant in the drama, other times you're a witness to it. Meeting Scotty gave us both a front row seat.

Not long after Terry moved in with Shani and me, Helen and her family moved out of The Castle. Two other men moved into their old place but did not take over the building management duties. Me, being nosy, decided to go next door to introduce myself. The door was opened by a man standing about 6 feet, 5 1/2 half inches tall. I introduced myself as his next-door neighbor and Terry's girlfriend. He introduced himself as a Staff Sergeant Scotty. I don't recall his last name, but he said he was a Marine and had done two tours in Vietnam. Terry was also a Vietnam vet. Terry had been a "rat": the ones who went into underground tunnels to weed out the Vietcong.

Scotty invited me in to have a seat and asked if I wanted a beer. "Cool," I said. As Scotty was in the kitchen, I noticed a photo album on his coffee table. I thought it was a family album, so I picked it up, and as soon as I opened it, there was Scotty in a jungle with a bunch of other soldiers wearing camouflage and holding pairs of severed hands. Other pictures showed them with ears on their belts. That photo album contained pictures of the real horror of war and what it can do to young people.

I remember thinking how Karenga thought that dancing and singing and making women feel like shit and the seven principles were the deal. No, Scotty and Terry were the real deal. Real warriors. Scotty and I became very good friends, and he taught me a few things. Next to the book the *Art of War* by Sun Tzu, he taught me more than anyone. Scotty was ruthless and he wasn't afraid to die. He challenged everyone except Terry. He had great respect for Terry. He also had respect for me.

One Sunday afternoon, Scotty and Terry had come into the house while I was cleaning my gun, a .38 caliber revolver. Shani was napping in the bedroom, and I was sitting on the couch, half watching something on TV, when I needed something from my purse. I couldn't find it; I didn't usually let my purse get so junky, and after cleaning it out I decided to clean off my pistol too. My father had given me the revolver years ago after the torture and that second rape, and I carried it with me everywhere I went.

Scotty walked in and tried to rag on me, asking me if I knew what I was doing with a big grin. Before I could rag back Terry spoke up and told him, "She might break it down faster than you, Blood." When Terry said that, I didn't say a word. I just looked at Scotty, winked my eye at him, and went back to cleaning my gun. We all laughed. It was through hanging out with Scotty that I began to think that maybe, possibly, I could find a way to direct the wrath that had been bottled up inside me all those years.

Another Saturday afternoon, Scotty came by looking for Terry. Terry had left a couple of hours earlier and I didn't know when he'd be back. So, Scotty asked me if I wanted to take a ride with him. I said sure since Shani was with her dad Perry. I grabbed my purse and scurried into the car. He was going to see a "somebody" about "something, somewhere." I didn't ask Scotty about his business, I just went along for the ride. Turns out, we ended up in a housing project in Watts. I stayed in the car while he went inside of a unit, and out of the corner of my eye, I saw three or four guys walking in my direction. They stopped, right at the porch of the unit Scotty had gone in. I looked at them and they looked at me. I didn't think anything of it. Once Scotty came out, he had words with one of the men. I couldn't make out what was said but it didn't sound like an argument. Scotty turned his back and started towards the car and the guy he had been talking to went into the house. As Scotty gets into the car, the guy he had words with comes back out, yelling. That's when Scotty looks at me and says, "You got my back, right?" I nodded yeah at him. I had no idea what was going on or about to go down, but whatever it was, I had his back.

As soon as I answered Scotty, the guy on the porch yelled something else. I turned my head to look at him when *BWAM! BWAM! BWAM!* Scotty started shooting from over the roof of the car with his .45. *OH SHIT!* I thought, turning and looking in the direction Scotty was shooting. Things began moving in slow motion; everybody scattered. Some of the guys ran back into the house; one guy ran around the side to the back, and another one dove onto the ground and just lay there covering his head.

POW! POW! POW! Without thinking too hard about it, I pulled my gun out of my purse and started shooting from the passenger side of the car. I didn't know who these guys were, so I didn't aim directly at them. I wasn't trying to kill them, just get them off of us.

"We need to go!" I yelled. None of the guys had shot back at us, but just because they didn't have guns on them at that second didn't mean there weren't any guns nearby. Common sense told me that somebody was about to come from somewhere and start shooting.

Scotty slowly and calmly got back into the car. He looked at me with a sly smile, said "Be cool," and started to slowly drive off. And you know what happened? Nothing. No shots, nobody running or driving after us. Nothing. I didn't say anything. I kept my cool like he said, but inside I was thinking *WOW.*

We stopped at a liquor store on the way back home, and when we got to The Castle, instead of going upstairs, we sat on the steps in front of the building. It was a nice, warm afternoon. We sipped from some beers and chuckled about what had just happened. I knew better than to ask Scotty a bunch of questions, but to be honest, I really didn't care that much. I really didn't care for the "why" because I was intoxicated with the "what." I felt a rush letting off that .38 and pulling the trigger until all the bullets were gone. Those particular gang bangers hadn't done anything to me; they didn't know me personally. I had no argument with them. But seeing them scurry like that, watching them run and yell to get away from us, was a kind of turn-on for me. It was like, "That's right, don't mess with me or I'll fuck you up!" It was powerful.

I guess I was able to do to those gang bangers what I hadn't been able to do to Karenga.

I didn't tell Terry the details of what had happened that afternoon, only that Scotty had taken me on an "escapade." I knew he and Scotty would eventually get together, and if Scotty told him, that would be fine. But I didn't think that I necessarily needed to be the one to offer up to my man that I had been shooting at some gang members in Watts.

I felt like I could trust Scotty. He was obviously fearless, and I began to think he was the perfect weapon to help me with a secret mission: find Karenga and exact personal justice.

That's what I was thinking at the time. Within my own madness, I thought Scotty's madness—because that's what it was . . . madness— was a good thing. But how could that be true? How could madness ever be a good thing? It never could be.

Scotty would eventually disappear. I have no idea where he went or what ever happened to him. All I know is that one day I was in my living room and heard a loud banging on a door. I went and looked through my peephole and, in the hallway, there were all these men at Scotty's door. When he opened the door, they took him. No going inside, no packing of bags; one just grabbed Scotty by the arm and they all left. I went to the hallway window and looked down, and there in front of the building was an unmarked van: no tags, no license, no markings, no nothing. These men all got in the van with Scotty and the van pulled off. I never saw or heard from Scotty again. I always believed that Scotty was a mercenary for the Marines, and they came to ship him off to a secret mission in another country. But I never found out.

In 1978, we moved to a bigger apartment off 107th Street in Inglewood. When I moved into The Castle it was just Shani and me. So as not to burden Perry financially, I only got a one bedroom. Even when Terry moved in, we kept the one bedroom instead of opting for a two bedroom. When she stayed with Perry, Shani had her own room there. Once we moved to Inglewood, Shani finally had her own room with us. Two daddies spoiled my Princess. Her room was a child's dream. I painted a mural of different animals that covered three of the four walls. Even though many girls wanted pink rooms, not my Shani; she wanted a soft orange with greens. She had a real brass bed, her own stereo system, her own color TV. The most beautiful bed set, beautiful rugs, anything she could think of Terry got it for her. Terry also furnished our apartment with custom-made glass pieces like a coffee table and a pyramid-shaped bookcase. *Everything* was custom-made. We were so happy in our new home. I thought we were happy.

The thing about self-medicating, other than calling an addiction like alcoholism or drug use self-medicating, is that everything becomes a reason to partake. Happy? Celebrate with a drink or a joint. Angry? Calm yourself down with a drink or a joint. Stressed out from your job, or your child, or your man? Wind down with a drink or a joint.

So yes, my drinking continued. I could've been what people refer to as a "mean drunk," but by that I think people usually mean someone who is just obnoxious and irate and, well, mean around other people. My meanness was cool. It was never really showing out in a social setting. It was more of a calculated thing. I'd get drunk or high, or both, and then I'd think about things, things that made me angry. And then I'd plot and plan. Sometimes I'd recognize what I was doing and say to myself "Girl, you ain't gon do that," or "Stop that silliness and go on about your business." Usually, I wouldn't follow through on any of my thoughts, and I wouldn't blow up publicly. But there were one or two exceptions.

I could tell that Terry was seeing another woman. Women can usually just tell these things. Long before we get the actual proof, we know. We just do. So that was already weighing on my mind. Then Terry started staying out overnight. Those overnights became more frequent, and I was angry about it. Very, very angry. Sometimes he'd explain himself, sometimes he wouldn't. After a while his explanations began to sound like he wasn't putting in any effort, just telling me *any* old thing.

In addition to being hurt, I felt disrespected, like he could just take me for granted . . . that I wasn't important, that I was just *there*. I had been thinking about how I was going to confront Terry about him cheating on me. One of my new neighbors I had become friendly with, Wanda, came by one night. I opened the door, and when Wanda saw my .38 in my hand she freaked out, asking what was going on. I told her I had been sitting on the couch, staring at the door, waiting for Terry to get home. "Oh girl! Wait a minute please!" she said and hurried back to her apartment. She came back and gave me some Valium and asked me to please not do whatever it was I was thinking about doing. I took the Valium and went to bed. Terry was spared from whatever I had on my mind that night.

One day, I'm in my kitchen with the window open, and I can hear some neighbor near our apartment talking about me. I didn't associate with them, so why are they talking about me? I told my Shani, "Wait right here, mommy will be right back." I went down the stairs, then went up the neighbor's stairs, kicked in the door, and started beating the woman up. Her husband came to pull me off of her and I gave him a couple of licks too. "Keep me and mine out of your mouth," I screamed. I went back down the stairs, back up my stairs, grabbed my daughter in my arms, and held her close as I called Perry, her dad, and told him "Come get Shani. I'm going to hell, and I can't take her with me. I've got to do this alone."

I was mad at Terry. I was just mad at the world. And another person, who had nothing to do with the reason for my anger, took the brunt of it. Perry didn't mess around with a bunch of questions or try to talk me out of anything once I called him. He came right over, and

I gave him our daughter. I knew how much he loved her and that he'd do anything and everything to keep her safe. That was the day I went to hell. I gave up the one person I truly loved unconditionally. I felt like I was losing control over myself. I was damaged and destroyed. And plus, my husband was having an affair. Or maybe I ran Terry off. I started drinking heavier every day, I kept on smoking and getting high. I just didn't care what happened to me or what I did to other people.

I eventually confirmed that Terry had been having an affair. The woman he had been seeing showed up at our apartment, pregnant, looking for him. This time I didn't get angry. Not with her I didn't. "You can have him," I told her, and proceeded to give her as much of Terry's clothing and other belongings as I could stuff into a garbage bag. Once she left, I immediately called a locksmith to come over and change the locks. I decided I wasn't going to fight over any man. No, not I. And Terry decided he wasn't going to fight for me either. I was numbed by the whole thing, so I just carried on.

Once the locks were changed, I attempted to move forward and get back to my routine. I'd get up in the morning and go to work. And I'd drink and get high. Before the week had passed, however, I came home to an empty house. Terry had gotten in and taken the rest of his clothing and belongings, as well as all of the furniture. *I mean all of it.* Terry had everything custom made, so I guess he reasoned it was all his. The only things left in the apartment were my clothes and a bar of soap. A third chapter in my life was now closed: first Perry, then Shani, and now Terry. There wasn't enough room for despair, so what else could I do? I started partying, adding that to my self-medicating routine.

Back when I was living at The Castle behind Manual Arts, I had gone out to a club one night with Vivian, the daughter of the building managers. We went to Jewel's Catch One nightclub up on Pico. The Catch One was a well-known gay spot, and Vivian was a lesbian who was dating the owner at the time. Anyway, we met a gay couple there, Johnny and Teddy Ray. Johnny was the more manly of the two, and Teddy Ray was the feminine one. I think nowadays they call them "top" and "bottom"? Anyway, Johnny and I hit it off and were close while I lived at The Castle. He lived in Inglewood also, and I ran into him one day while grocery shopping. We started hanging out together. Once Terry left me with nothing but a bar of soap, I called up Johnny and he took me in. This was around late 1979 or early 1980.

Johnny liked to party, and I was okay with that. The partying helped push my anger issues back down beneath the surface. That's not to say there was no drama involved, though. There was plenty of it. Then again, maybe they were just escapades?

Johnny met all kinds of people, and I would tag along with him as often as I could. One time, he was invited onto a party yacht for a cruise going to Hawaii. I assumed it was just for the weekend, but I didn't ask, and I wasn't told. I simply said yes when Johnny asked me. Everything was paid for; there was no money coming out of my pocket, so why not? There was alcohol and weed onboard, which was all I needed!

The yacht left from Long Beach, which is south of LA. I stood on the top deck, marveling at how blue and peaceful and wide and magnificent the Pacific Ocean was while a small live band was playing on the main deck. I wandered around, not really mingling but acknowledging people, drink in one hand, joint in the other. I finally sat down in a cozy chaise lounge chair next to two guys on the main deck. I wasn't really paying attention to them, then one of them said something that made my ears perk up like one of those little dogs you see: cocaine. I didn't mess with cocaine. Didn't want to be near it or anyone who messed with it. One guy said something about "the coke" and the other one said the "bricks" were down below. *What have you gotten yourself into now, Alice?* I said to myself. I saw a rabbit hole coming towards me that I did not want to be a part of. I had no interest at all in going to prison, and that's what cocaine meant to me. Even though weed was illegal at the time, I felt it was really harmless. But cocaine? That was considered a hard drug, like heroin, and to me that meant hard time in prison, which I had no interest in.

I started getting anxious and imagined the worst-case scenario: The Coast Guard would get a tip and follow us out to sea. They'd pull up next to us, ask to board the boat, find the cocaine, and I'd be hauled off to jail in handcuffs with all these other people. And because I wasn't rich like all of them, I'd be left to rot in jail after they all made bail. I tried not to panic, but I found Johnny and told him I needed to get the hell out of there. Johnny calmed me down for the rest of the cruise to Hawaii. Once we docked, he helped me catch a flight back to LA.

Did I overreact? Maybe. Weed, alcohol, and paranoia are *never* a good mix.

Another time I was hanging with Johnny and a friend of his named Gerald, and we all dropped acid. That's what it was called in the '60s when you would ingest LSD, a psychedelic drug. You would take these really little pieces of thin paper, about the size of the tip of your finger, and place it on your tongue. The paper would dissolve, and the LSD wound enter your system and, eventually, you'd start to "trip out." Again, I thought it was harmless even though it was illegal. We went tripping down Santa Monica Blvd., dancing and laughing. I was hearing music, but it was all in my mind. We were laughing and dancing along the boulevard somewhere near the Hollywood Freeway when I looked around and saw Johnny and Gerald had lagged behind me. I had gotten way ahead of them, so I waited for them at a bus stop, still dancing and laughing. Some prostitutes were there, and they were laughing at me and encouraging me along. I was in my own world, having a great time, waiting for Johnny and Gerald to catch up, when this Rolls Royce pulled alongside the curb. The women ran up to the window to get the attention of this man sitting in the back seat, but he pointed and said, "I want her," talking about me!

This Arab gentleman with his chauffeur tells me to get in, so what do I do? I got in! I'm in a good mood, laughing and smiling, always in search of a party. Anyway, he starts propositioning me, saying let's go to the Beverly Hills Hotel, where he's staying. We can do this, that, and a third. How much do you need and want for your services? I was high, but I wasn't that high. I smiled as I pulled out that .38 and pointed it at him. I told him, "Sir? I am not a prostitute. I am a robber." By this time Johnny and Gerald had caught up to me and were looking in the window. "Take care of the chauffeur," I told them as I took the man's wallet and watch. Johnny grabbed the car keys from the ignition while Gerald stared the driver down. I jumped out the back seat and we all started running for our lives. We ran a few blocks until we saw a bus, hopped on, and rode back to Inglewood. All told, we made out with about $4,000 as well as jewelry.

There were other escapades during this time. Most of them occurred while I was under the influence of one substance or another. But underneath those influences was rage. Wrath! Anger!

I was still angry about Karenga and what happened to me. He had been paroled from prison to San Diego. He didn't even serve his full ten years. He was just out and about and two hours away from Los

Angeles.

I was so angry.

Angry about the times I didn't listen to my intuition when I was in Us. I had wanted to be of some help to the women in the organization, so I stayed instead of leaving.

I was angry that I wasn't able to free myself and Idili from that garage even though I was the Nzinga of the Matamba.

I was angry that I didn't blow up Karenga and Tiamoyo right after it happened like I wanted to.

I was angry that I was raped again, and even though I didn't know for absolute that sure it was my apartment manager, I was angry I hadn't shot him anyway.

I was determined never to be a victim again. I decided that if anything was going to happen, I would be the victimizer and not the victimized. I just didn't care anymore. I was killing myself slowly.

I had already tried to kill myself once before, not long after we were tortured when I was about twenty-one or twenty-two. It was at The Castle one day when I was home alone. I had been drinking and I was frustrated that I couldn't get to Karenga. I was just tired, and so I tried to slit my wrists. I still have the scars on them. Then I realized that I didn't want Perry and Shani to find me like that. I ran cold water over my wrists, bandaged them up, and hid them under long sleeves while they healed. I never told Perry about that. His presence in my life was vital, but even he still wasn't enough. All the partying and drinking and smoking was numbing me, but it was also killing me slowly. And I knew that's exactly what it was doing.

12

STABLE (?)

I was grateful that Johnny had taken me in, and we had some wild times, but I knew I needed a change. I wanted to move out of his apartment and get my own spot, but at the same time, I had this feeling that even that wouldn't be enough. I needed something *really* different.

This was the mid-1980s. Still self-medicating, I started looking for a job that wasn't in sales. I looked through the want ads in the paper and saw one that shouted at me: a group called Greenpeace was hiring for travel to Alaska. They were an environmentalist group. I knew nothing about environmentalism or Alaska, but I loved to travel, and I had good organizational skills and nothing to lose. My daughter was no longer my responsibility; she was being taken care of by her father. Travel and the money sounded good, so I went to their office in downtown LA for an interview. When I got there, I was a little bit shocked. They were all hippies! I was like, "Okay, I guess this is the hiring crew?" But I was wrong, the whole organization was hippies!

Two days later I was hired, and a few days after that I arrived in Anchorage and was wowed by Alaska's beauty. My employment was to be a minimum of six months where I was supposed to collect water, air, and oil samples. I would observe the environment and the animal wildlife and write reports. My parents had always told me it was a world out there waiting for me. My family traveled a lot when I was a child, but I had never lived elsewhere. Alaska was a good break for me, but I left after six months. I was still drinking and smoking while I was there. After my own stash of marijuana ran out, I relied on the hippies for theirs, and of course, I could get alcohol. I wasn't dating anyone, so there was no relationship drama to speak of. It was solitude, but it was loneliness too. Alaska was cool but I just never could get used to that twenty-four hours of sun for the whole six months, day or night. *24 hours?* I just couldn't do it. I quit and caught a plane back home.

Once I got back to LA, my mom told me that Terry had been looking for me. My mom liked Terry because he was handy and knew how to fix things. She never liked Perry that much even though I thought he was cool. I moved back in with my parents temporarily to figure out how to get my life together. While there, Shani would spend time with me, which I loved, but I didn't want to take her back. I felt she was safe where she was with her father. But Terry wanted to get back together. That didn't interest me. Once it's over, it's over. But my parents wanted me to get married to him. Once again, not listening to my own spirit, I went ahead, and Terry and I got married in a little church in Inglewood. We got another apartment in Inglewood; it was actually a back house on Budlong near 106th that belonged to a friend of Terry's.

So now we're officially married, but Terry is still being unfaithful. I put up with that crap for about a year, then I was out. There were less of my antics involved this time. I just left him and that was it. I was through with him again, but he wasn't through with me; Terry began to stalk me. This was around 1982 or such. I still knew I needed some type of change, and now I had a stalker, so what did I do? I left LA and went up north to the Bay Area.

I didn't know anybody when I went up north. I had known someone years ago, but they were no longer there. I went to Hayward and got a motel room and started looking for a job. I found a multiracial private school in Oakland that was looking for a teacher. I didn't have a degree or a credential at the time, but education had always been my interest, so I went and talked with the owner of the school, a Jewish man. He hired me, and once I started teaching there I moved to Oakland.

When I finally had enough money saved, I moved from that motel in Hayward to downtown Oakland near the waterfront. That's where I met Felix Mitchell.

Felix Mitchell controlled much of the drug trade in Oakland and the Bay Area. He made his money in heroin first and was the man to go to in the early beginnings of the crack era. He was also considered to be a folk hero to many because he provided income and made donations to community programs. He would take the money he made from selling death and destruction and give it back to the community. Of course that's a contradiction but what are you gonna do?

Felix had more money than he knew what to do with. Houses, apartments, cars, clothing, jewelry, parties, and giving back to the community. The police finally caught up with him and he was sentenced to life in prison, where he was killed. His funeral was just as lavish as his life had been: his Rolls-Royces (yes, more than one) were part of the funeral procession in addition to limousines. His casket was in a horse-drawn carriage. *Thousands*—and I mean thousands—of folks paid their respects as he was taken through the streets of Oakland one last time. That's how huge the contradiction was. This drug dealer was treated like a head of state. I guess he was the head of state for Oakland. But before all that happened, I was a neighbor of his in an apartment building on the waterfront.

I didn't know he was paying attention to me. I didn't even know who he was at first because I was brand new. He knocked on my door, and he was trying to impress me with a fur coat, but my thing is not dope dealers. At the time, I didn't know who he was and I didn't like him. He wasn't my type romantically, but we did become like friends. He showed me what crack did to people.

To give you an example, he had judges and lawyers as his clients. He told me he had a couple of their wives involved also. The wives of judges and lawyers, they, too, would be on crack or working for him. It was wild! One time, a couple of them would even drink the water that he was mixing the crack with. They would drink that. I saw this with my own eyes, and he was telling me what other things they would do for it. It was like a lesson he was giving me: "You need to stay away from this." He kept a couple of pit bulls in his apartment, and once, I hate to even say this, he smeared some dog mess on a shoe and had this judge lick it. He was a real cold person.

I stayed in the Bay Area till the late '80s and life was better for a while. I eventually became the director of the little school where I had been working. My money was good, so I treated myself. I didn't drive, so I bought myself a motorcycle. When I wasn't going to work, I would ride my motorcycle throughout the East Bay Area: Richmond, Berkeley, Concord, Hayward, San Leandro. I called it my "wind therapy" and it was great.

Riding was thrilling. I rode pretty regularly until I had an accident. My motorcycle slipped in the rain once and I scraped my face. This was during the days when you didn't have to wear a helmet. But I wore everything else! I wore a leather jacket, pants, gloves, and boots because those things helped with wind and cold and in case you did get into an accident.

When I was younger, around the time of the torture, I was into motorcycles for a bit. I used to hang out with the Chosen Few, a Black motorcycle club started in South LA back in the 1960s. My parents had a neighbor named Mr. Kenny who lived with his wife Miss June, but he had two daughters from his first wife who would come visit, Rosie and Peaches. They were in the Chosen Few and invited me to come to their dances at their club on Manchester and San Pedro. I would go sometimes, but I wasn't interested in joining the club. I enjoyed being around the motorcycles, and after somebody let me try theirs, I went and bought my own. That was my first experience with wind therapy and I loved it!

I bought myself a small older-model motorcycle, a Harley, and I would ride on my own or sometimes with the Chosen Few. There were a few guys in the club who liked me, but this was not long after the torture, so I wasn't thinking about romantic male companionship. I wanted to hang out and ride and smoke weed, which is the main reason I got my own bike. I would never get on those guys' motorcycles with them; that was a no-no. That was part of the unspoken protocol in the club at the time: If you were riding on the back of a guy's motorcycle, and you weren't his wife, there were "expectations" of you. This was a no-no to me. Rosie and Peaches were considered "Mamas" in the Chosen Few. "Mamas" had something to do with sex, and I wasn't going there. I refused to ride on the back of a man's motorcycle. A Motorcycle Mama was somebody's woman and I'm nobody's woman.

Anyway, riding that bike after the torture, and later in the Bay Area, sort of took me back to my childhood. Our father would ride bikes with us when we were kids. Those were good times. I needed the feeling of that memory again.

13

ASCENT

I didn't dream of being a teacher when I was a little girl, but educating children became a passion of mine once I got close to graduating high school. I knew I was an African nationalist and wanted to be a revolutionary since I was at least nine. I loved to read and explore and travel. At some point, I wanted all Black children to do that also. I wanted them to expand their minds. I saw how so many of my friends and people I went to school with had never gone anywhere, how their minds were stuck. I wanted better for us.

I had the opportunity to go to UCLA, like a lot of other kids from South Central LA in the late '60s, but I dropped out once I joined Us's dance troupe and started traveling and never finished. Once I got that job in Oakland at that private school, it was a chance to do something great: to mold young Black minds. That's what I wanted to do. I left Oakland and returned to LA. It was the late '80s and I was in my late thirties. I was still damaged, I was still self-medicating, but I also had hope. I hoped I would be able to make a difference.

I got back to LA, found a little apartment with my savings, and started looking for a job where I could teach. I was back living in Inglewood, and one day I was having lunch at a Pizza Hut, right at Manchester and 11th Avenue, off of Crenshaw Blvd. I looked across the street and saw a preschool and went over to check them out. They weren't hiring for teachers at that time, but they needed a cook and

I figured that would get me in. *A preschool . . . Maybe I can get some experience,* I thought, because I hadn't had any experience with children that young.

It was run by a woman named Anne Pernell and her husband. After I got the job, I started taking some classes at Southwest College in child development. When I got to fifteen credits I was able to teach the children. I was officially hired as a teacher! I really had fun there for eight years, from the late '80s until the mid-'90s. One major thing I did was put on plays with the children. They performed Mary and Joseph coming from Watts and Jesus and Zulu warriors were from there. The parents wanted me to travel with the children doing this particular play. Ms. Pernell and her husband owned two schools, the one in Inglewood and another one near 48th Street and Crenshaw. After the students performed their plays, I became the director of both schools.

That was really cool! I worked there for eight years, but what I really wanted? What I really wanted was to teach at Marcus Garvey Elementary School. Marcus Garvey was the main independent Afrocentric or African-centered school in South LA. I really wanted to teach at Marcus Garvey because it fit me. Duh!

The Marcus Garvey School was on what we called the "West Side" of South Central LA, which was basically West of Western Avenue. Anyim Palmer, the founder, was a product of the segregated school system in the South. But he was nurtured and educated by teachers who challenged him because they were part of the Black community. He wanted to do the same thing for other Black children. He was a college dropout who went back to school and got all the degrees and titles one would need to teach children, and then he started his own independent school in 1975.

Once I had child development credits and preschool teaching experience under my belt I went down to the school and talked to Dr. Palmer. He was like, "Yes!" I got hired and would be teaching fifth grade students. I thanked Ms. Pernell and her husband and told them goodbye. This was around 1994. I was excited, but I would be gone in less than one year.

Anyim and I clashed over the development of the children. I wanted the children to be able to exercise their creative side and Marcus Garvey was only academic, period. I never knew this. I wanted more creativity in the curriculum. They'll give the children a jump rope and give them thirty minutes and then it's right back to class, but that's not good for the whole child's development, you know what I'm saying? They need play time and time to just be creative, to paint or color and draw, to perform the kind of plays I had put on. We clashed over that, and Anyim fired me.

Now, at the time, I did not know that Anyim Palmer had had a relationship with Karenga. He mentioned it when he brought me to his office to fire me. I want to say that I believe I had heard that elsewhere, later on, but I do remember the two had been good friends back in the '60s but had a falling out. That didn't surprise me. I could see that because Anyim had a strong personality. It was his school, so it was his way or the highway. And of course, Karenga being the egomaniac that he was, yeah, I could see that perfectly. I could see that friendship coming to an end.

Anyway, Anyim offered to help me find another job with some folks he knew who were into recycling Black dollars; he wasn't a complete hard-ass. But I didn't want another job in another field; I wanted to teach children. So, I told him, "I'm going to take my class with me."

The next thing I knew parents were actually taking their kids in my class out of Marcus Garvey and I had twelve little boys. That's how I started a school in my apartment. I got all my supplies from the 24th Street Elementary School. They had a program where they were doing home studies and provided materials, and I took it from there. I had a school right there in the living and dining areas of my apartment in Inglewood that I shared with my then-boyfriend Janoris Bryant.

Twelve little boys, and we went from fifth to seventh grade in two years, 1994 to 1996. We would have class in my apartment, and then I would load them into Janoris' car, and we would go to Manchester Park for their physical education.

But after '96 we had some problems. We had to move because the owner of our apartment building sold the property and the rent went up. I was still smoking during this time but I wasn't drinking as much. We moved to a nicer spot in Inglewood that we also eventually had to leave.

I started the school again in the new apartment, this time with six little boys, but I wasn't making enough money, and neither was Janoris. The rent was pretty hard.

I ended up having to stop the school. A lot of those parents really were disappointed because they really wanted me to teach their children. It was just too much going on at that time, not between me and Janoris, but money-wise. So, we ended up moving to Palmdale.

Palmdale is about an hour from LA, sixty miles north. I remember we were driving out there and had to pass through the Angeles National Forest to get there. This area was where Karenga told his men to take me and kill me in 1970.

Palmdale is a real desert town. All of LA is a desert when you really think about it, but because we have Hollywood and the Pacific Ocean right here, we don't really think of LA as a desert. Palmdale is a desert: dry, dusty, cactus trees, and a type of palm tree unique to the area. Lots of racist white folks out that way too, but a lot of Black folks also found their way out there beginning in the mid to late '80s. They were running from what the crack epidemic was doing to South Central. It was also very cheap to get a house out there. Black folks who could not afford to buy a house in Los Angeles, even though it was South LA, could buy one in Palmdale. They could be homeowners out there, but it would be an hour away from family and friends they had grown up with.

We stayed with Janoris's brother when we first arrived. We eventually got our own place, and I started working at this church that was African-centric. They had a preschool across the street, and the lady that hired me was named Ms. Ruby Martin. Ms. Ruby dealt with the foster care system out there. She had been there for a long time and knew everything there was to know about the system.

The church that ran the preschool was Catholic but African-centric. I had no interest in the church whatsoever because even though it was African-centric, it still had too much European Christianity in it. The irony of this is that Palmdale is where I met my faith.

How did I meet my faith? Without making the story too long, my daughter Shani had been angry with me for several *years*. Angry because I had given her to her father to raise. She wanted her mother, and I was nowhere to be found. Or when I was found, I wasn't asking—or telling—her to come and live with me. So she resented me a lot. To the point where we're no longer mother and daughter. We were just two women, and there was a man in between us.

Shani and my supposed boyfriend Janoris began an affair.

Shani was so angry from not having a mother and I understood. I didn't wanna be a part of the "baby mama drama thing," so I stayed away and let Perry and Shani's stepmother raise her, and they did a good job. She was a cheerleader and doing whatever children do, you know. She wasn't with me going through the dope trip and all that. So, yay. But children get angry. The Word teaches us to "honor your mother and your father." Yeah, true, but don't bring your children to wrath either. We do that without even knowing, see, because we are into us, you know, ourselves.

Meanwhile, that child is the one that's looking. And so Shani didn't have anything to look for toward her mother, and the mother is a very important role: the nurturer. So, my daughter hated me for a long time. She loved me but she hated me. Love and hate, that type of thing. Thin line, you know. And she did something to get even with me. She never knew about the torture. She didn't find out about that until much later, when she was almost thirty or so. I had never told her what happened to me.

I can't tell you all the emotions and words involved in this. But it was another trauma. It was very traumatic for me.

I moved out of the apartment with Janoris and now I was homeless. I didn't know anyone I could stay with in Palmdale, but I damn sure wasn't going to stay in that apartment one second longer. The church ran the preschool, and they said they would help me, but they didn't. It was some gang members that helped me. The gangsters that I would buy my weed from invited me over to their home. They treated me like a queen. They really did.

I told them, "You know, I'm just frustrated. You know, I'm just beyond . . . I mean, it just keeps happening, you know, like when is this gonna end? My daughter hates me. She's gonna keep my grandson away. I mean, she's my only one." So in that, the gangsters told me, "You live with us." I was treated like a queen, and I stayed with them about a month or so.

While I was at the gang members' house, they introduced me to another Deborah Jones. Another woman with the same name. Basically, I was homeless, and she needed to spend some time in LA and asked if I wanted to stay in her apartment while she was gone. Of course I said "YES!"

I got dropped off at her apartment by those gang members. As they were leaving, one of the guys hands me some weed and he says to me, he looks me in my eyes and says, "Ms. D, God has got something better for you." I was like, "I don't want to hear all that. Just give me the weed and the drink!"

I was ready now! I had a place all to myself, I had my weed and my drink. I was just about to start my pity party right there in that other Deborah Jones's apartment when I heard this voice. Something inside me spoke and said, *"Deborah, daughter of Judah. Come from among them."*

Now, my family has mental illness. My sisters and my father. I thought I had escaped it, but when I heard that voice it scared me. I thought, *It's finally got me too!* But that voice said "De-BO-Rah," which is the Hebrew pronunciation of my name. It's how those Jews up on Fairfax pronounce my name.

When this inner voice so gentle called me "De-BO-Rah," I was like, "What?!! No!" I turned on every light in the apartment. I thought I was going crazy. And I was scared. I mean Karenga, none of that scared me like that. I was in a corner shuddering, and the voice said, *"Come from among them De-BO-Rah, daughter of Judah."*

That's when I started to study the Bible, right then and there. The woman had a Bible on a bookshelf, and I picked it up and started reading. I'd never done that before. My parents are not religious, they never went to church, none of that. I got a revelation out of reading the Bible. I was able to see in a mirror like that, and it helped me a lot. I looked at the Bible, not the white man's Constantine stuff. Who we really are, from Adam, from the very nature of him himself.

I had an awakening. I dumped the weed and the Hennessy, all of it, in the sink.

I stopped everything I had been doing. I stopped drinking. I stopped smoking. I stopped doing it all, right then.

That's the path I chose and I've been at peace ever since.

I haven't looked back.

That weekend when I was tortured, I thought I was going to die. But Karenga gave and then rescinded that order to kill me. So, despite my fear, I walked away to live and fight another day. No one can tell me there isn't a higher power.

14

AFTERWORD

My life today? I'm at peace, okay? I'm not religious. I'm spiritual. I had an experience and it helped me to become . . . I stopped using the word "best." I started using the word "better," okay?

And I'm continuing to get better, and better, and better. And I'm at peace inside where it matters the most. Everybody around me can be chaotic, but I'll just get up and go to my room and close the door, you know?

I reconciled with my daughter Shani, and we enjoyed several good years together before she unfortunately passed away June 23, 2021. I'm a grandmother and a great-grandmother twice over. I'm an Auntie and a friend. I'm at a place where my health kind of stopped me from working with children and doing certain things, but I don't dwell on it. I've had two spinal surgeries and was told I'd never walk again; the scars from the surgeries look almost like I have a zipper on my back. I still live with the pain of what happened to me Mother's Day Weekend 1970, but I'm here! I'm optimistic, you know, about everything. And I have hope where I didn't have any. And I see brighter things than I thought I would see when I see young people at the age of nine who own businesses, when I see them speak at age eleven, which we didn't have that opportunity. We're those same children of today. No difference. We just didn't have that opportunity to be on TV. These children have an opportunity to expound on how they feel and everything. So, I see hope.

I went through a hard, hard, hard time, through the fire to come to the other side. And I learned this: that adversity is good. It builds character. Now, while you're going through it, you don't realize that because you're angry, you've got all the emotions involved. I know better, perhaps more than a lot of people, but I'm saying at my age now, it builds character. But that's a completely different thing than forgiveness or someone thinking they are entitled to violate you. *No one is entitled to that. No one has that right.*

What is the most important thing I would say to young people today, especially women? Lots of important things I would say. One, always listen to your intuition. Always. I don't know why we don't trust ourselves. Why we don't trust our intuition, that little voice that tells us something is not quite right. Our intuition is on our side! It wouldn't steer us wrong the way so many individuals out here in the world will. I had to learn the hard way to believe in myself and the little voice that was on my side. If you're in an organization and you think something is off or wrong about a situation, it probably is. You can investigate further to confirm your intuition—be careful—or you can just leave. Either way, your intuition means you no harm. Others might, but not your own intuition.

The other thing I would say is, be careful with anger. My anger almost killed me.

Uncontrolled anger, misplaced anger is dangerous to you and others. We can end up striking out at those closest to us: those close to us personally or just those close to us physically. Perfect strangers might get the brunt of your anger and they had nothing to do with what made you angry.

Be forgiving towards yourself. Despite not listening to my intuition, my gut, a few times, I had to forgive myself. I was very young and didn't have enough life experience to even know which times to listen to my intuition. I do now. Listen to yours before it gets too late in the game.

And lastly, never give up. Keep going, even when you don't know where you're going; have faith that you will land okay.

ACKNOWLEDGEMENTS

Deborah Jones

To my King and Messiah, Yashua. My dad Frank Jones, who cared for his family and supported us in all our endeavors. My mom Mildred Faye Jones, who was my queen and wanted me to reach higher levels. My daughter Shani, who taught me to reach for righteousness's sake. To my grandson Cha, being a better and better dad for Chosen is part of your legacy. To the Tom and Ethel Bradley Center at California State University, Northridge, and to Kumasi, thank you for standing by me. Many thanks also to Susan, Feb, Tina, and Sarah and Diane. To Perry, you were my lifeline. Thank you.

Thandisizwe Chimurenga

I thank Deborah Jones for allowing me into her life and sharing her truth with me. It has been an honor. Many thanks to her daughter, Shani Maisha Scott (rest in peace), and Shani's father, Henry Pierson (Perry) Scott (rest in peace), for sharing with me also. I am indebted to the Black Power Archives of the Tom and Ethel Bradley Center at Cal State, Northridge for putting Deborah and me together, and to OGs Kumasi and Bird for their years of service, dedication, and wisdom. I am grateful to Dr. Kwasi Konadu for his steadfast support. Dr. Kimberly McNair, and "my sista from anutha mista Nana Gyamfi" also provided invaluable support, for which I am truly grateful. I appreciate the many former members of the Us organization who shared their memories with me. Lastly, but most importantly, I thank my Ancestors and the Almighty Creator for their Love, Support, and Protection. Asé.

www.ingramcontent.com/pod-product-compliance
Lightning Source LLC
Chambersburg PA
CBHW060528080526
44586CB00012B/656